Gettysburg
Colorized

90 Battlefield Photographs Transformed into Color

by
Jack Kunkel

Modern View from Cemetery Ridge

Copyright

Table of Contents

Copyright ii
Table of Contents...iii
Forward v
Map Overview..vii
1   The Photographers.. 1
2   Fighting on the First Day 3
3   The West Side of Gettysburg 13
4   Town Central 21
5   South Gettysburg 29
6   Little Round Top..39
7   Devils Den..47
8   Slaughter Pen 57
9   Trostle Farm & Emmitsburg Road..63
10   Rose Farm 71
11   Culps Hill 83
12   East Cemetery Hill...89
13   Cemetery Ridge...97
14   The Cemeteries 103
Index...109

Forward

Those interested in the history of the battle at Gettysburg are fortunate that there were many photos taken on the field and the town shortly after the battle - in many cases, just a couple of days later. But of course all these photos are in black and white, and black and white images usually don't hold our interest like color images do. (When's the last time you watched black and white TV?) Right or wrong, black and white photos usually look distant - something that happened long ago and far away. It takes color to really make photos pop and bring images to life. We spot details in color that we often miss in black and white. It's possible of course to simply paint over the old photos, but that would destroy their underlying texture - the all-important shading and tones. Variations in shading and tone are what makes a photo a photo. Painting over a photo might make a beautiful painting, but it covers the underlying photo, including the hundreds or even thousands of small shading details. Even the most intricate painting can never contain the detail of the simplest photo.

THE TECHNIQUE

The good news is that Photoshop, a software program, now offers a technique to colorize black and white photos, and by "colorize," I mean that color is added to the photo *without* disturbing the underlying texture or shading. The photo looks just like it did in black and white, except now it's in color. Photoshop makes colorization fairly easy to do, even for non-technical inclined. The bad news is that it's not as easy to apply as just pushing a button. It requires painting every detail in the photo, just like regular painting, except with a digital paintbrush. As already mentioned, photos have a lot more detail than paintings, and colorization means that every item that appears in the photo - every blade of grass, every leaf and limb, every hair, every rock and fence post - has to be hand-painted (colorized) using the digital paintbrush. So colorization is not for the faint of heart and it requires a decent knowledge of Photoshop, at least at our current stage of technology.

But that's the process I applied to the photos in this book, and if you buy this book you can honestly tell your neighbors that every photo in this book has been hand-painted!

THE "RULES"

It's my book so I get to make the rules. There are only two:
1.   Don't paint what's not there.
2.   Focus on reality, not beauty

I rarely added anything that wasn't in the photos. For example, almost all the skies in the original photos are "blown out" (white). On the landscape photos, I could easily have dropped in some gorgeous sunsets and sunrises that would just make your mouth water. And it was tempting to at least add some clouds, or the sun, or whatever, but I didn't because I would be guessing as to whether it was a sunny or cloudy day. Rather than guess, I left all the skies a bland blue. B-o-r-i-n-g, I know! But better I thought than manufacturing a fake sky. I did on occasion add some leaves and grass to the photos where it was obvious that's what was there, but I never added or subtracted any people or landmarks (boulders, houses, etc.).

Along those same lines, I avoided making the scenes too vibrant, too pretty, which is easy to do in Photoshop. In fact, in some cases I could have included fake leaves and grass that would have looked better and more real than what was in the grainy photo. But I usually didn't. The goals were always to colorize the photos as close as possible to what the scene probably looked like at the time, while still remaining true to the actual photo image. Sometimes those two goals conflicted and I had to make subjective decisions, but I tried to keep them to a minimum.

COLORING DECISIONS

Some of these photos, even many of the originals, are in bad shape. Often I spent as much time restoring the photo and figuring out exactly what I was looking at, as I did in actually coloring the item. (Is that a blanket on his body or just his pant leg? What's that thing on the side of the road? What color where his or her eyes and hair? What color was her dress?)

Often I was reduced to guessing, but wherever possible I did my research. I can for example tell you the color of dirt in the Gettysburg area, the colors of Union and Confederate uniforms and insignias, the colors of women's dresses and men's suits of the time. (Having researched women's dresses, my junk email is now filled with advertisements for women's dresses). Sometimes the original building in the old photo is still standing, or the actual boulder is still there, and in those cases I used the actual colors, taken from a modern photo.

However some things still stumped me. For example, I never figured out what colors people painted their houses back then, other than white, or what color roofing they used.

So it's up to you to decide if I made the right color decisions, and to send me hate mail if I got it wrong. But the whole idea is to make you forget that these photos were ever in black and white in the first place.

In any case, these photos are never finished. There's always something to improve on each of them, either in the restoration or in the colorization. Maybe someday the technology will improve, or maybe I'll discovered better base photos, or maybe my skills will improve. But right now, this is as far as I could take them.

Photo Sources

If the original photo is hazy, the colorized result will be hazy, unless the photo can be restored. But really bad photos can't be fully restored. So when colorizing it's important to use the best photo available, preferably the original, as the base photo, Most of the photos in this book came from the Library of Congress, As far as I know, those *are* the original photos, although some of the Library of Congress photos themselves came from books. As a last resort, in a few cases I had to settle for copying my base photo out of books (there's no legal restrictions on photos that old), but I would have much preferred to be working with the originals, which will always be the sharpest.

If the photo came from the Library of Congress, I didn't mention it in the photo's caption. But if it came from elsewhere I usually mentioned that. In all cases, whether they came from the Library of Congress or elsewhere, most of the photos needed restoration work; sometimes a *lot* of restoration work, before the colorization even began.

Special Thanks

Back in the 1970s, William Frassantino taught at Gettysburg College. He was interested in Civil War photography, especially Gettysburg and Antietam photography, and he did ground-breaking work in discovering most of the locations where the original photos were taken on the battlefield. Over the years he wrote several books on the subject. As far as I'm concerned, he's still the Man when it comes to locating the original sites of photos, and interpreting the circumstances of the photo. I mention Frassantino here because I refer to his deductions quite often in the book

The Other Book

One of my previous Gettysburg books (A Gettysburg Photo Tour: Before & After Photos), which I'll call "the other book," has many similarities to this new book, but also some important differences. This new book is not a replacement or a new edition of the other book. For example, the other book includes the period photos and their exact locations, including GPS coordinates and detailed maps, along with a modern photos of each location. It's still a better choice if you plan to actually tour the battlefield. And because it's in black and white, it's also cheaper!

This newer book contains many – not all - of the same photos that are in the other book (but also some new ones), and often the same commentary. But this book is different because it spends little time focusing on the exact photo location; rather it concentrates on bringing the original photos to life in living color (An odd word choice, given the numerous death scenes).

Some of the commentary is indeed exactly the same as in the other book but, freed from discussing directions on how to find the exact photo location, often I've expanded on the commentary to discuss specific details brought out by the colorization, or just to add some new thoughts. Also of course, this new book is in full color, and therefore more expensive.

My Credentials

The last time I was in Gettysburg, standing around Devils Den making notes and looking important, some elderly lady (about two days older than me) came up and asked "If I was an expert or something." Even though this is my third Gettysburg book, I didn't know what to tell her, and I still don't. A Gettysburg expert? Compared to what? I don't have any degrees in history, I've never been a Gettysburg guide, and I've never done first-line research into musty letters and manuscripts - though I'd like to do the latter if I had time.

So I don't consider myself a *real* historian. Instead, I consider myself a "splainer." I take the research that's already been done, which probably includes about 99% of everything that will ever be known about the battle, condense it down, and dispense it in a manner that's intelligible to non-experts without putting them to sleep. I'm also a technology buff and I make full use of technology to bring the Civil War to life, such as colorization in this case. Bottom-line, in my opinion most the research on Gettysburg has been done. Excluding happenstance - meaning somebody finds some unknown photos or letters in Aunt Mary's attic - further enlightenment on the Civil War battles will not come from research, but from advances in technology - such as hopefully this book.

Anyway, that's my story and I'm sticking to it.

If you purchase this book, I hope you enjoy reading it as much as I did writing it.

Jack Kunkel

Map Overview

Below is an overview of the portion of the field covered in each book chapter, and their chapter numbers. This map is not a guide to the entire battlefield. The photographers of the day only photographed certain portions of the battlefield, and therefore the photos and chapters in this books follow that same pattern.

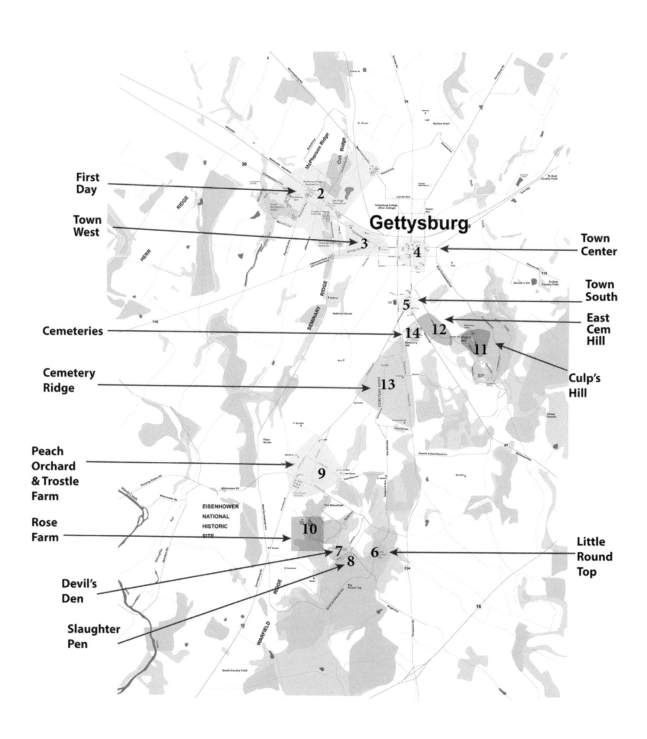

1 The Photographers

The original photos in this book didn't just pop up on our coffee tables. Somebody had to go out in the field and take the pictures, dealing with the smells, the elements and the bugs, using the crude photo equipment of the time. The men who took these photos were pioneers, experimenting with the art and science of taking outdoor photos in the middle of a civil war. Although they strived to give viewers the impression that the photos were taken in the heat of battle (sometimes even using posed scenes), no photos at Gettysburg, or any Civil War battle, were taken while the battle was in progress.

It's helpful to have some background of who these men were and how and when they took their photos. And the two photographers who particularly stand out when it comes to Civil War photography are Alexander Gardner and Matthew Brady.

Alexander Gardner

Although Matthew Brady's name is synonymous with Civil War photography, many of the more famous photos of Gettysburg - including all of the death photos - were taken by Brady's nemesis, Alexander Gardner. It was also Gardner who took the famous death scenes a year earlier at the Antietam battlefield. Gardner was also Lincoln's personal photographer, and he took the famous photos of the Lincoln conspirators and their subsequent hanging in 1865.

Gardner once worked for Brady, and it was while in Brady's employment that Gardner took the death scenes at Antietam in September of 1862. These photos shocked the nation and were a tremendous financial success. But it was Brady's studio and the photos went out in his name, with Gardner receiving little or no credit and probably not much of the compensation. No doubt for that reason, in May of 1863, two months before Gettysburg, Gardner established his own studio, in the process luring away two of Brady's top employees - Timothy O'Sullivan and James Gibson. Unlike Brady, Gardner was careful to give credit to O'Sullivan and Gibson for their photos, which is probably how he convinced them to join his studio.

Brady's main studio was in New York, 210 miles from Gettysburg, whereas Gardner's studio was in Washington, just 77 miles from the battle. So upon hearing of a great battle at Gettysburg, Gardner and his crew had a head start.

Based on painstaking analysis by William Frassantino, it appears that Gardner and his associates spent the night of July 4th in Emmitsburg, Maryland, about 10 miles south of Gettysburg. They reached the battlefield about 5pm on July 5th. It would have taken at least an hour or more to set up the photo equipment, so the earliest they could have commenced taking photos was 6 or 6:30pm. Night fell at 7:24pm on that day. So if they did any photography on July 5th, it was minimal.

Therefore, most of the Gardner death-photos were taken on July 6th. By then portions of the Army of the Potomac were already departing Gettysburg, chasing Lee.

Amazingly, three entire days after the battle, Gettysburg residents had not yet discovered the tour-guide business. And so Gardner and his crew probably wandered the battlefield pretty much on their own, getting directions and advice from Federal militia guarding burial details of Confederate prisoners.

The last elements of Lee's army departed Gettysburg via Hagerstown Road (today, Fairfield Road) on the morning of July 5th. Beginning that day, the Union army collected all loose weapons on the field and then set about burying the dead, starting from the north end of the field and working south. First they buried the Union dead, and then the Confederates. So the last bodies to be buried were Confederates on the southern end of the battlefield.

Given the sensation created by his death photos at Antietam, Gardener was determined to photograph dead soldiers. Fortunately for him, he just happened to approach the battlefield from the south, where the last dead remained unburied.

Bottom-line, all of Gardner's death scenes had to be taken either late on the 5th or on the 6th, because by the morning of July 7th, the Army of the Potomac had departed Gettysburg, with the burials completed. And, with one possible exception, all the death photos were taken on the south end of the battlefield, specifically around Little Round Top, Devil's Den and Rose Farm.

The one possible exception pertains to some photos of dead Union soldiers in an unknown location, Somehow, somewhere, but most likely as Gardner approached the battlefield up Emmitsburg Road, he happened upon some as yet unburied Union dead, but it's a mystery as to where and when he did so. It's likely the Union dead where the first photos he took on the battlefield. From there, Gardner likely moved on to photograph the Confederate dead south of the Rose farm, and from there he headed over to Devil's Den.

Probably camping near Devil's Den on the evening of the 6th, Gardner's crew was likely put out of action for the next couple of days due to rain and cloudy skies, making outdoor photography difficult or impossible at that time. He next surfaced at East Cemetery Hill, where he was the first of legions of photographers to take the obligatory shot of the Evergreen Cemetery Gate. Probably by then growing antsy to get back to Washington with his precious death scenes, he hung around town long enough to take some rather mundane shots of Gettysburg buildings. But that was it. On the morning of July 9th Gardner and his associates departed for Washington, no doubt intensely pleased to have scooped their former employer, Brady. But in their rush, they skipped taking any photos west or north of town, or of Culp's Hill, the Peach Orchard, the Wheatfield or Cemetery Ridge. Possibly they weren't aware of the importance of these locations so soon after the battle or more likely, they knew there were no more bodies there to photograph.

Matthew Brady

About a week after Gardner's departure, Brady and his photographic crew reached the town, probably around July 15th or 16th. There being no bodies to photograph by then, Brady concentrated his shots on significant landmarks and panoramas. Unlike Gardner, who had to rush to get his shots before bodies were buried, Brady could take his time. Partially for that reason, Brady's shots are all well composed, with consistently sharp, detailed backgrounds. And no doubt he had a local guide by then, who escorted him to the best spots.

Brady's eyesight was bad and he didn't actually take the photographs himself, instead leaving that up to his unnamed assistants. But he was in charge.

Even though he could take his time, Brady, like Gardner, neglected to take any photographs of Cemetery Ridge, the Peach Orchard or the Wheatfield. And for some odd reason, he didn't bother taking any photos of the highly photogenic Devil's Den, which would have been in his full view from Little Round Top.

Brady probably departed the field around July 23rd at the latest.

Local Photographers

Although Gettysburg and the surrounding area had some local photographers at the time of the battle - particularly the Tyson Brothers, the Weaver Brothers and Frederick Gutekunst - they were studio photographers, unequipped to take outdoor photographs. Thus it took a couple of weeks after Brady's departure before the local photographers obtained the necessary equipment to venture outside.

Their photos over the following months and years have given us valuable additions to what Gettysburg looked like at the time, with numerous photos of town buildings, the interior of Evergreen Cemetery, Rock Creek, and more.

Photography Equipment

There were two main types of camera equipment at the time:

1. Plates - A large single plate camera equipped to handle 8X10" glass negatives. These would produce today what we would probably call a large print photo.

8X10 Glass Negative Plate opened & closed

2. Stereo Photos - A twin-lens camera produced double-images which could be viewed through a set of goggles, much like the 3D type goggles you might occasionally see today. Stereo photography was popular at the time of the Civil War and for decades thereafter.

Developing a negative had to be done on-site in a dark room or, in the case of outdoor photography, inside a dark wagon. The process usually took about 10 minutes per negative.

Stereoscopic Viewer, used to view photos in stereo, giving a 3D effect. The photo on the right is a typical example of a stereo photo.

2 Fighting on the First Day

Fighting raged on the first day of the battle of Gettysburg both north and west of town, but only the area west of town received any photographic attention in the days, and even the decades, following the battle.

WHAT HAPPENED

By late June, 1863, the Federals were desperately trying to locate Lee and his army, which were on the loose somewhere in Union territory - maybe heading farther north into Pennsylvania, maybe heading east to Philadelphia, or maybe even Washington. Confederate cavalryman J. E. B. Stuart was already raising hell in the Washington area. Lee sightings were reported everywhere, and the Lincoln administration was approaching a nervous breakdown.

Union cavalry commander Brig. Gen. John Buford was assigned the job of finding Lee's army. Buford and his division reached Gettysburg on June 30th. His scouts and locals reported Rebel contact to the west, For some reason - call it cavalrymen's intuition - Buford was positive the Confederates would approach the town from the west the next day, down Chambersburg Pike. To buy time and allow Union infantry to reach the field - especially that excellent defensive ground on Cemetery Ridge south of town that he had noted on his arrival in Gettysburg - Buford deployed his dismounted cavalry in a series of skirmish lines along the Pike, with his main and final line located on a shallow rise called McPherson Ridge, named for a farm located there. Sure enough, the next morning the van of Lee's army, a Confederate division commanded by Maj. Gen. Henry Heth, came marching down Chambersburg Pike where it soon encountered Buford's troopers.

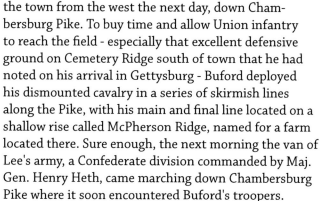

John Buford
1826 - 1863

Heth assumed he was dealing with some pesky Yankee militia, and routinely began pushing the Federals back. But the resistance stiffened, and Heth finally realized that he was facing cavalry, not militia. Still, cavalry was no problem for his veteran infantry. So Heth just pushed a little harder, and gradually his men drove the Federal skirmishers

Henry Heth
1825 - 1899

back to Buford's final defense line on McPherson Ridge. At almost the last moment, Union infantry reached the scene. The foot soldiers from the Union I Corps, commanded by Maj. Gen. John Reynolds, had been trudging up Emmitsburg Road south of town when they heard the firing. Soon they were ordered to cut across fields, jogging past a Lutheran Seminary while still loading their weapons. Out to the west of the seminary, across the fields a couple hundred yards, they could see the cavalry's gun smoke on a ridge - McPherson Ridge. It was a case of the infantry coming over the hill to save the cavalry as the foot soldiers quick-timed over to the ridge, where they replaced Buford's troopers and clashed with Heth's advancing infantry. So now the two infantry heavyweights collided, raising the roar of the battle to ever-increasing heights. Neither side intended to be pushed off that field.

John F. Reynolds
1820 - 1863

Reynolds was soon killed, but that had no effect on the spreading battle. Both sides shoveled infantry into the conflagration as fast possible, creating the inferno forever known as The Battle of Gettysburg.

The Confederates first arrived from the west on Chambersburg Pike, but soon more appeared from the north on a rise called Oak Hill. Now McPherson Ridge was ablaze from one end to the other. But by mid afternoon the exhausted Union forces had been pushed back to Seminary Ridge (called Oak Ridge north of Chambersburg Pike). Disorganized and with their backs to the town, the Federals made a desperate stand on this second ridge, but eventually Southern forces overwhelmed them and drove them in disarray back through the town, toward a redoubt southeast of town called Cemetery Hill.

Photo 2A   Chambersburg Pike at Willoughby Run

View looking NW toward Herr's Ridge. Photo probably taken by Tipton sometime in the 1890s.

This is the road used by Lee and two of his three army corps in their approach to Gettysburg. The other corps approached from the north at Oak Hill, which is to the right of the camera. You're looking northwest as Chambersburg Pike descends at Willoughby Run (a creek) before ascending toward Herr's Ridge. Gettysburg is about a half mile behind you. The photo was probably taken by Tipton, sometime in the 1890s.

Although this photo was taken 40 years after the fact, it doesn't look like much could have changed here since 1863. That's a toll house on the right, but probably not the same one that was on this road during the battle; the original I believe was on the left side of the road. The house was definitely not there at the time of the battle. This road was considered good road, good enough to pay for the privilege of using it, from at least 1863 to the 1890s.

The camera's standing on McPherson Ridge, where Buford's cavalry formed it's final defensive line. From the top of that rise on Herrs Ridge, all the way back to the camera, the dismounted troopers had been fighting a delaying action against Confederate infantry, which was trying to push its way into Gettysburg. Cavalry seldom fought toe-to-toe with infantry, for good reason, but Buford was trying to buy time for the approaching

Union infantry to reach the high ground - Cemetery Ridge - on the southeast edge of Gettysburg.

From Herr's Ridge the approaching Confederate division commander - Henry Heth - was mildly perplexed that Yankee cavalrymen would challenge his veteran infantry. He ordered his two leading brigades to peel off: Archer's Brigade to camera left and Davis' Brigade to camera right - and form battle lines to deal with the stubborn horsemen. Meanwhile he set up his artillery on Herrs Ridge. Just as the Confederate skirmish line was advancing up this rise, Union infantry arrived, and the battle exploded into an inferno.

Visible on the left atop Herrs Ridge is Herr Tavern, with the barn of the Crist farm appearing in the right background. Both the tavern and the farm were there at the time of the battle. Herrs Ridge was used as a Confederate staging area for subsequent attacks throughout the 1st day's fighting, and artillery on the ridge would play on Union forces with deadly effect throughout the day.

Today if you visit Gettysburg, you'll find manicured, low-cut grass on both sides of this road. But as you can see from the photo, things didn't look like that at the time of the battle; these were farm fields, filled with crops, fencing, and trees.

Photo 2B   Herbst (McPherson's) Woods - looking south
Photo taken by Brady & Co., around July 15th, 1863

Matthew Brady took this photo with two plates, intended as a panorama. That's him posed beside the fence.

On this south side of Chambersburg Pike, the infantry fighting began in those woods on the morning of July 1st, 1863, just two weeks before this photo was taken,. The Iron Brigade, a crack unit in the Union army - rushed into those woods (often incorrectly called McPherson Woods, but a farmer name Herbst actually owned them), from camera-left to camera-right. Somewhere in there, probably about where that dead tree is in the photo, the Federals collided with Tennessee and Alabama infantry of Brig. Gen. James Archer's brigade, advancing in the opposite direction. The Confederates had just crossed a creek - Willoughby Run - which is where the trees drop lower on the right. The Confederates got off the first volley, dropping about a third of one Federal regiment, but the survivors stood their ground and answered with their own volley. The woods exploded in smoke and flame, and the battle of Gettysburg was on.

Col. Roy Stone's Pennsylvania brigade - called the "Bucktail Brigade" because of the buck tails they wore on their caps - reached this area and formed up on the right flank of the Iron Brigade, Stone's 150th Pennsylvania regiment occupied a line from this pond to the tree line.

The Federals fought off the attacking Confederates and in fact drove them in disarray back across Willoughby Run, even capturing the Confederate brigade commander, Archer. But more of Lee's men were arriving. Shortly after noon the Confederates rallied and attacked with overwhelming force. In this location the Bucktails were hit by the 44th and 55th Virginia regiments. The Federals fought hard, but were slowly pushed back (camera left) to a Lutheran Seminary on the western edge of town, where they made a desperate last stand. Finally, around 4pm, the entire Union line crumbled and fled through Gettysburg to Cemetery Hill - which was the "good ground" Buford had saved for them.

Except for a modern Park road cutting through it, this section of the field hasn't changed much today. The little pond is still there. No doubt soldiers of both armies used it to fill their canteens.

Photo 2C McPherson Farm Photo taken approximately July 15, 1863 by Brady & Co. View looking NE. Photo owned by Gettysburg National Park.

This is a shot of McPherson Farm, which sits atop McPherson's Ridge. There was heavy fighting in and around this farm on the first day of the battle. Col. Roy Stone's Union brigade, which included the 143rd, 149th and 150th Pennsylvania regiments, soon joined by the 6th Wisconsin of the Iron Brigade, occupied the farm for most of the day.

This photo, probably taken around July 15th, less than two weeks after the battle, looks northeast toward the (out of view) Chambersburg Pike, and just past that, the Railroad Cut; both of those areas were heavily contested during the fight. The distant tree-line is Oak Ridge. The Confederates attacked this farm from the direction of the Railroad Cut as well as from the west, to the left of this photo. Eventually the entire Union line collapsed and the Confederates occupied this area for the remainder of the battle.

The owner of McPherson Farm, Edward McPherson, resided in Washington DC, renting out the farm to 40-year-old carpenter and tenant-farmer, John T. Sletz and his wife and five children. At the start of the battle the family fled the farm and took shelter in the basement of the nearby Lutheran Seminary.

Though they look fine in the photo, the barn and house were severely damaged in the fighting, requiring three months to repair. If you look closely, you can see there is damage to the side of the house, where a board props up the wall which looks badly scorched.

During the fighting approximately 200 wounded, mainly Union, soldiers were carried or crawled to the shelter of the house and barn, where they remained with virtually no care until the Confederates departed early on July 5th.

The house was repaired and remodeled but was destroyed in a fire in 1895. The barn was also remolded, but not to the way it looked at the time of the battle. It was eventually brought back to its original look by the Park Service upon William Frassantino's discovery of this photo.

Just as Stone's brigade arrived at the farm on the morning of July 1st, Sgt John Shafter of the 143PA found a crock of "sour milk," (buttermilk), in the cellar of the house. He carried it to that wagon shed, where he and others ladled the milk to their mouths with their filthy hands. The brunch ended abruptly when a Rebel shell crashed through the shed's roof.

The two people in the photo are Matthew Brady (standing) with one of his assistants or guides. In the blowup photo, you can see two militia soldiers sitting in the wagon shed. (Maybe they found that bucket of buttermilk!)

Closeup photo. Note the two soldiers sitting inside. They're militia.

Photo 2D The Lutheran Seminary Photo by the Tyson Bros. in August, 1863. View looking NW.

This is one of the many photos taken of the Lutheran Theological Seminary after the battle. Unfortunately all the photos, including this one, show the Seminary's *front*, which faces east toward town. But it was *behind* the Seminary, facing west toward McPherson Ridge, where the Federals made their last stand before being driven across these grounds to Gettysburg and Cemetery Hill.

The Seminary, built in 1832, was and still is one of the most prominent structures in Gettysburg. Cavalry commander Buford observed the battle on the morning of July 1st from that cupola, and he was there when Maj. Gen. John Reynolds, acting commander of the Union army, rode up the Seminary lane from the right of this photo and called up to Buford in his perch.

Once the Confederates seized this location, Lee undoubtedly used the same cupola to observe Cemetery Hill. His tent headquarters was just a short walk to the right of this photo on Chambersburg Pike.

The Seminary served as a hospital for two months after the battle, which was about the time this photo was taken sometime in August. Gettysburg residents later wrote of arms and legs being tossed out the Seminary windows.

The Seminary sits atop of what most visitors and history books call *Seminary Ridge*. But Seminary Ridge is actually just an extension of Oak Ridge to the north, and only derived its special name after the battle. Many locals still consider the whole ridge to be Oak Ridge.

Photo 2E *View from Northern side of Herbst Woods* Looking SE toward Seminary Ridge.
Photo taken by Brady & Co. around July 15, 1863.

In this photo, taken less than two weeks after the battle, we see Matthew Brady with someone - probably a hired local guide - pointing toward Herbst Woods (aka McPherson's Woods) and the vicinity where the acting Union commander at the time, Maj. Gen. John Reynolds, was killed early in the first day's fighting.

The view, taken just behind the McPherson barn (out of view on camera-left), faces southeast toward Seminary Ridge. In the left-center distance you can see the Seminary cupola over the top of the treeline.

After bloody fighting throughout the morning and early afternoon, the Union line cracked around 4pm, with Federals retreating to the Seminary where they made a last stand. In the process, the 150th Pennsylvania, which had been stationed around McPherson Farm, very likely retreated across the cornfield you see here. One of the 150th's color bearers, Sgt. Samuel Pfiffer, turned at the far edge of the field, waved the American flag and shook his fist. Confederate Lt. Gen. A. P. Hill, observing through his binoculars, noticed Pfiffer (whose name Hill discovered later). Hill scanned the field elsewhere and when he returned his gaze, he noted with regret that the defiant sergeant was down, and as it turned out, killed.

After the battered Union forces were driven from this field, they fell back to the Seminary where they lined up behind a thin barricade constructed that morning by Buford's cavalry. But the Federal infantry had plenty of artillery support. Now brigades of Confederates advanced across these fields toward the Seminary, through a storm of canister and rifle fire which decimated the Southern ranks. But finally one South Carolina brigade - Col. Abner Perrin's - managed to curl around the left flank of the Union line (to the right of the Seminary in this photo) and roll-up the entire Union line, sending its survivors fleeing through Gettysburg and on to Cemetery Hill.

One thing you have to say about the Army of the Potomac: it was tidy. On the evening of July 1st, this area would have been covered with the broken bodies of dead and dying men ("as numerous as pumpkins in a field") and artillery horses. But now, less than two weeks later, after the exhausted Federals policed-up the area before pursuing Lee, the place looks peaceful enough for a picnic.

In fact those woods were often used by locals for picnics.

The field past that cornfield must have been loaded with graves. Oddly, neither Gardner nor Brady took any photos of grave sites anywhere on the battlefield.

Photo 2F   Looking west toward the Oak Ridge Railroad Cut

Photo taken by C. J. Tyson in 1867 . Photo owned by William Frassantino.

Here we're facing west with Gettysburg at our backs, looking toward the Oak Ridge Railroad Cut, fours years after the battle.

There were two railroad "cuts" involved in the first day's fighting at Gettysburg, where the newly built railroad line sliced through both McPherson and Oak Ridges. At the time of the battle, the tracks had not been laid. Today, tourists flood the McPherson Ridge Railroad Cut, while completely ignoring this Oak Ridge cut. This is not surprising since the McPherson Ridge Cut is on the Park tour map, and Oak Ridge's Cut is not even mentioned. Also, in 1990, the National Park Service and Gettysburg College made a land trade which, for whatever reason, resulted in the partial destruction of the northern face (the right side) of this Oak Ridge Cut.

During the first day's fighting, Oak Ridge served as the final defensive line for the Union I Corps. The railroad cut here resulted in a gaping hole in the middle of the ridge, thereby assuming vital tactical importance because its capture would have allowed the Southerners easy access to the rear of the I Corps line. So at midday on July 1st, Lt. James Stewart's Battery B, 4th US Artillery, supported by infantry, deployed at the top of this cut, straddling the banks on either side to protect the entrance.

By 4pm, the Union line on Oak Ridge collapsed and the only protected escape route was this unfinished railroad bed, which leads eastward into town. Thousands of Federals frantically streamed through this gap toward this camera position, and on into Gettysburg and eventually Cemetery Ridge. "We had the Yankees like partridges in a nest, and the only way they could get out was up the railroad," according to one Southerner.

Fighting ended here at around 4:30pm when two Confederate battle lines - Lt. Gen. A. P. Hill's from the south and Lt. Gen. Richard Ewell's from the north - converged on either side of the cut, capturing 400-500 Federals, the largest single haul of Federals prisoners in the battle.

Stewart's battery continued blasting onrushing Confederates until the last possible moment, trying to buy time for the escaping infantry. Stewart finally pulled out with the loss of two guns, having sustained the second highest casualties of the 68 Union batteries in the three-day battle.

Lee's headquarters was just a 100 or so yards to the left of this photo on Chambersburg Pike (see Photo 3A). When the pre-attack bombardment commenced on the climatic third day, Lee walked over to the northern side of this ridge and watched the Alabama battery there, the Jeff Davis Artillery, as it shelled Cemetery Ridge.

Photo 2G Lee's Headquarters at the Thompson House

Photo taken in 1866 by the Weaver Bros. View looking N across Chambersburg Pike.

Late in the afternoon of July 1st, after his troops seized the field in brutal fighting, Lee and his staff trotted up Chambersburg Pike to this house on the western edge of Gettysburg. At the time it was owned and occupied by a widow, Mrs Mary Thompson. Situated near the crest of Seminary Ridge and along the main western artery leading into town, the spot was a good location for directing the battle, so Lee set up his tent headquarters just across the road from where this photo was taken.

Lee held staff conferences and ate several meals here at this house, although (just in case you're wondering!) his personal tent was actually pitched on the opposite side of the Chambersburg Pike, now a parking lot. Either out of respect or intimidation, Mrs. Thompson treated the courtly Lee as an honored guest. She commented on his gentlemanly deportment, but complained bitterly of robbery and property destruction by some of his aides.

She also didn't care much for J. E. B. Stuart, describing him as a man "rough in his manner and cruel and savage in his suggestions." She was present but did not hear the conversation when Stuart showed up at her house late on July 2nd to face an angry Lee, who presumably rebuked him for not reaching the battlefield sooner. Late on the 3rd day, after the failure of Pickett's Charge, she saw Stuart and Lee meet again, and this time she heard

the frustrated Stuart urge Lee to shell and destroy the town before they retreated, and to display the black flag (take no prisoners). She said Lee replied that they had never done so before, and they would not do so now.

It's usually assumed that the woman posing in the photo in the long dress is Mrs. Thompson. But especially in viewing the photo in color, it's obvious that there's another woman in the photo, wearing an apron and remaining discreetly next to the house.

It's possible the woman in white is indeed Mrs Thompson, and the two men and the woman in the apron are her hired-help to repair her house. But it seems just as likely that the woman in the apron is actually Mrs. Thompson, and the woman posing is a prominent tourist or an important politician's wife.

The house is still there to today. Note its stone construction; there's at least five or six different kinds of stones used in that building, which must have been expensive to quarry and fit to the walls. Bricks would have been cheaper, but the owner chose stone. Many of the farms around town were large, two-story buildings. Gettysburg was quite prosperous, at least by the standards of Confederate soldiers, most of whom hailed from hard-scrabble farms in the South.

Photo 2H   Confederate prisoners on Seminary Ridge
View looking SE across the grounds of the Lutheran Seminary. Photo by Brady & Co., around July 15th, 1863.

These characters, Confederates heading to prison camp after the battle, are making the most of their photo-op, pleased to have their pictures taken by idiot Yankees so dumb they didn't even know what Southerners looked like.

Notice how lean they are. Obesity was seldom a problem in the Southern army, or in the Union army either.

They're well attired for Confederate soldiers. For one thing, they all have shoes, possibly stripped off dead Yankees; they didn't walk all the way from Virginia in those shoes. Excluding weapons and rations, they're equipped with everything they need to live in the field for months - canteen, blanket-roll, poncho, tin cup and haversack. Most Confederates considered a backpack to be an unnecessary luxury; instead they carried a haversack - about the size of a large purse - into which, wrapped in rags, they usually stuffed some greasy salt pork - usually tinted blue; some weevil-infested cornbread fried in grease; a spoon and fork; tobacco, pipe, and flint; a razor and piece of soap; cartridges; and a letter or picture from home.

For food they depended upon the company supply wagon. But on those numerous occasions when the wagon was empty or unavailable, the half-starved soldiers had to forage for their supper, often after a hard day's march. They became experts at foraging (farmers tended to call it *stealing*), and the Southerners gorged themselves in the fat, Pennsylvania farm country, which was in stark contrast to the war-ravaged Virginia countryside. This photo was likely taken around July

15th, less than two weeks after the battle. Frassantino speculates that these were stragglers snared in Union mop-up operations somewhere along Chambersburg Pike or Hagerstown Road (aka Fairfield Road), Lee's line of retreat.

The camera location is directly off of Chambersburg Pike. The Lutheran Seminary is just out of camera range on the right. Brady was probably taking a photo of Lee's headquarters at the Thompson House located 50 yards behind the camera, and happened upon these prisoners, or maybe they happened to be marching by. They were likely part of the 2,500 Confederates marched off to Union prison camps the following day, July 16th. No doubt Union guards were just out of camera range.

The Park or Seminary has a plaque here stating that the barricade, now stone, was erected on July 4th by Robert Rodes' division. That may be true, but this photo clearly shows that the barricade was built of heavy lumber, not stones. The lumber probably came from the Oak Ridge railroad cut, which was still uncompleted at the time of the battle, and located about 100 yards off to camera-left.

Frassantino pin-pointed this photo location by the background view, particularly that tall tree on the left, which he knew from another photo to be on Cemetery Ridge around the time of the battle.

Outdoor photography was still a novelty at the time, and nobody knew exactly how to pose. So each of the trio chose his own pose.

2A

Originals

2B

2D

2E

2C

2F

2H

2G

3   The West Side of Gettysburg

What Happened

By the morning of July 1st, the van of the Army of the Potomac, the Union I Corps, was still on the south side of town, marching up Emmitsburg Road. As they neared Gettysburg, they heard firing to the west of town. Soon excited officers ordered them to cut across fields at the double-quick toward a Lutheran Seminary, and a hundred yards beyond it, to a rise known as McPherson Ridge. There they became embroiled in a brutal, all-day battle with Lee's army.

Following the I Corps up Emmitsburg Road that day was the Union XI Corps, which took up positions north of town, in front of Gettysburg College, and on a hill known as Blocher's Knoll.

By mid afternoon, relentless Confederate assaults had smashed both Union corps. The I Corps, pushed back to Oak Ridge (aka Seminary Ridge), finally imploded around 4pm. The survivors fled in disarray through town, where they were joined by the equally wrecked XI Corps. Together the two streams of fugitives merged into a flood, seemingly guided by magnetic impulse toward a prominent height southeast of town called Cemetery Hill.

The Confederates, almost in as much disarray in victory as the Federals in defeat, stayed hot on the Yankees' heels as they fled through town. Frantic rear-guard fighting erupted in the town's streets, while terrified civilians huddled in their basements. The Southerners captured hundreds of Federals hiding in house attics, basements, and under porches and stairways, before halting at the base of Cemetery Hill where, awaiting them at the top, was the quickly reforming Union army.

A modern view of the McClean Farm from Oak Ridge and, past the farm, west Gettysburg

Photo 3A Chambersburg Pike looking W toward Tate House and Oak Ridge Railroad Cut

View looking west toward Seminary Ridge. Photo taken around August, 1863 by the Tyson Bros. Photo owned by William Frassantino.

Here, Gettysburg is at our back as we look west up Chambersburg Pike toward Oak Ridge (known after the battle known as *Seminary Ridge* to left of the Pike and *Oak Ridge* to the right of the Pike). That's the Oak Ridge railroad cut on the right, the same one seen in Photo 2F.

On the left of the photo you can see the Lutheran Seminary. Farther to the right along that white fence was the home of Dr. Charles P. Krauth, a professor at the Seminary. And just on the right side of the Pike, nearest the camera, was the Oak Ridge Seminary (aka Ms. Shead's School for Girls) a private school operated by Ms. Carrie Shead at her house (Photo 3B). Visible on the ridge and bracketing the Shead's house was the house and barn of C. Henry Dustman. The Mary Thompson's house, which Lee used as his headquarters, is just out of view beyond the Dustman house. Finally, that's Mr. Perry J. Tate's house (closest to the camera on the far right). Only the Shead house and the Seminary still remain today.

On morning of July 1st, excited townspeople gathered on the top of that ridge, eager to watch a scrap with the Rebs, unaware they were about to become part of it. Boys clamored up nearby trees to get a better view. But the Confederates on Herrs Ridge were still ranging their guns, (They didn't have much practice. Due to shortages

of ammunition, Confederate gunners almost never fired their guns except in actual battle).

Suddenly a Confederate overshot shrieked over the onlookers and crashed nearby, creating pandemonium. Boys rained down from the trees as the crowd raced back down this road. A lawyer named William McClean later admitted that the exploding shell "had the effect of utterly removing all the curiosity I had entertained, and I beat a hasty retreat, not in the best order either, to my home, where I found my wife and children in tears over my absence, and in fear for my safety."

As 10-year-old Dan Skelly, raced back down this road, a Union general and his staff galloped past him and, reaching the top of the ridge, turned left into the lane toward the Seminary. The Union infantry had not yet come up. Skelly always believed it must have been Maj. Gen. John Reynolds racing to the Seminary to confer with Brig. Gen. John Buford, who was then in the cupola at the Seminary. (Unknown to young Skelly, his older brother, Jack, lay mortally wounded at that moment in a hospital in Winchester, Virginia. (See Chapter 5).

This photo was taken just across the street from the John Burns' house (Photo 3F).

Photo 3B Ms. Carrie Shead's House
View looking N across Chambersburg Pike. Photo taken around 1865 by the Tyson Bros.

At the time of the battle this house, just across Chambersburg Pike from the Lutheran Seminary grounds, was owned by Ms. Carrie Shead, who operated a school there - Mrs. Shead's School for Girls, where young ladies learned good manners. But on the afternoon of July 1st, 1863, all hell broke loose when the Union line collapsed on Oak Ridge, and the house was caught in a flood of thousands of panicked Union soldiers streaming down the Pike, heading toward town (to the right of the photo).

One of these fugitives was Col. Charles Wheelock of the 97th New York. With Confederates right behind him, the colonel dodged into Mrs. Shead's basement. But the Confederates followed and, at the point of a bayonet, a burly Southern sergeant demanded the colonel's sword. Amazingly, Wheelock refused, causing the situation to grow tense in a hurry. Fortunately for Wheelock, just as the irate sergeant was contemplating running him through, more Union prisoners were herded into the house, momentarily distracting the sergeant. But he soon returned, again demanding the sword, but now the sword had vanished; Wheelock explained that another Confederate had seized it.

Sometime over the following two days Col. Wheelock escaped his captors. After the battle he returned to the house and recovered his sword. At the suggestion of Ms. Shead, she had hidden it in the folds of her dress during the chaotic scene in the basement.

Col. Wheelock wasn't the only Union soldier to make the trek back to Ms. Shead's School for Girls. Pvt. Isa Hardman of the 3rd Indiana Cavalry also returned - to marry Ms. Shead's sister, Louisa Shead.

Note the telegraph poles. They weren't there two years earlier at the time of the battle.

Photo 3C & 3D Looking east toward Town from Seminary Ridge Photo taken around August. 1863 by the Tyson Bros.

These two hazy photos form a panorama of Gettysburg, taken from Seminary Ridge looking east into town, just a month after the battle, Though the scene has changed considerably, the camera location is still quite accessible, being very near the Lutheran Seminary. The road on the left no longer exists. After capturing Seminary Ridge, as well as the town itself, a portion of the Confederate battle line extended through Gettysburg along the Hagerstown Road, seen leading into town from the right foreground (once west of town the road becomes Fairfield Road). Note the missing boards and rails of the fences along the road; they were probably stripped by Southern soldiers for use in their camp fires during the three-day occupation. Beyond the town and to the extreme left are the distant tents of Camp Letterman, a large tent-hospital set up by the Federals after the battle.

Photo 3E John Burns in front of his house. Photo taken around July 15, 1863 by Brady & Co.

John L. Burns, a cranky 69-year-old shoe-maker, was a character around Gettysburg long before the battle. Never shy about voicing his opinion on any subject, he was particularly against drinking and drinkers.

He, along with another man he detested, alternated as town constable - a make-work job provided by the town to give the older gentlemen some extra income. Because Burns took his duties seriously he was the constant target of pranks by the local youths, who delighted in having Burns chase them.

One thing Burns disliked more than drinkers was Rebels, and when Confederate Maj. Gen. Jubal Early's division briefly occupied the town about a week prior to the battle, Burns started smart-mouthing and making threats, prompting Early, something of a grouch himself, to order Burns deposited into the town jail until the Confederates left town.

On the morning of July 1st, the townspeople heard the rumbling of battle west of town. Now out of jail, Burns was itching to get into the action. Finally he couldn't stand it, and sometime around mid-morning he loaded up his ancient flintlock musket and powder horn (which he claimed to have used in the War of 1812), and wearing a stovepipe hat, a tie, and a long linen duster to keep from getting his clothes mussed, he set off to deal with the Confederate army personally, looking like a militant leprechaun.

According to several boys who were standing across the street from his house (255 Chambersburg Street), Burns spotted Joseph Broadhead, a "one-eyed neighbor." Burns invited him to grab a gun and come along. When Broadhead declined, Burns became "very abusive," calling him a "coward and chicken-hearted." Broadhead's wife now roared to the defense of her chicken-hearted husband, hollering at Burns. Hearing the commotion, Mrs. Mary Slentz popped out from next door and joined

the argument, rebuking Burns for his abuse of the neighbor and advising him to stay home.

Out-gunned, Burns stomped off alone up Chambersburg Pike, a solitary figure marching west toward the sound of the guns,

Along the way, Burns encountered a wounded Union soldier and asked to borrow the soldier's modern rifle. Now armed with a better rifle and cartridges, Burns next popped up in front of Maj. Thomas Chamberlin of the 150th Pennsylvania Infantry, requesting orders. At the moment the 150th was in the thick of the fighting around the McPherson Farm.

Maj. Chamberlin later wrote of Burns moving with deliberate step, carrying his Enfield rifle at a trail. "His somewhat peculiar dress consisted of dark trousers and a waistcoat, a blue 'swallow tail' coat with burnished brass buttons, such as used to be affected by well-to-do gentlemen of the old school about 40 years ago, and a high black silk hat, from which most of the original gloss had long departed, of a shape to be found only in the fashion plates of the remote past."

Not knowing what to do him, the harried major referred Burns to the regimental commander, Col. Langhorne Wister, who directed Burns to the Herbst Woods next to the McPherson Farm where he would find better shelter from the sun and enemy bullets.

Well, hell, he didn't come out here to sit in the shade! So he again headed toward the sound of the loudest firing and invited himself into the ranks of the 7th Wisconsin and 24th Michigan of the Iron Brigade - arguably the toughest brigade in the Union army, currently engaged in furious fighting in Herbts Woods. In short, he was on the front line of the Army of the Potomac in the largest battle of the Civil War, blasting away at the damn Rebels.

Three bullet holes later, including a serious wound to his leg, Burns lay helpless on the battlefield as the Federals were forced to retreat. Knowing that Confederates would not take kindly to a civilian carrying a weapon - in fact they might shoot him as a "bushwhacker" - Burns flung away his rifle and buried his cartridges.

When the Confederates found him, he gave them a sob story that he was a noncombatant, wandering the battlefield seeking aid for his invalid wife. After one of their surgeons patched him up, he apparently laid on

the field over-night; the next morning he crawled and hobbled to a cellar of the Henry Dustman house and lay there until the battle was over and the Confederates departed. Ironically, the Dustman house was within a stone's throw of the Mary Thomson house, Lee's headquarters during the battle. (See Photo 3A for a look at the Dustman house). Had Burns been healthier and gotten his hands on another gun, Civil War history might have been re-written.

After the battle he became a national hero. When Abraham Lincoln came to Gettysburg in November to dedicate the National Cemetery, he requested to meet Burns at the downtown house Lincoln was staying at (the David Wills House). Later, the two walked together and attended services at the nearby Presbyterian Church on Baltimore Street on November 19, 1863.

Burns in full battle dress

Photo 3F   John Burns on his porch

Photo taken approximately July 15, 1863 by Brady. View looking SE across Chambersburg Pike.

This is the earliest known photo of John Burns at his house in Gettysburg. Burns didn't actually own the house; he rented it from the off-site owner, Jesse D. Newman. The building was torn down around 1891.

The house was situated at the western end of Chambersburg Street, at what is now 240 - 242 Chambersburg Street, where that street joins Chambersburg Pike.

This photo, looking southeast, was taken at almost the same location as Photo 3A, which looks west up Chambersburg Pike, off camera to the right.

After the battle Burns became a celebrity and a steady procession of photographers dropped by to take his photo. Like every Gettysburg resident since, he quickly discovered the tourist trade, and began charging for

the privilege of being photographed. He always had a gun and sometimes a big hat as props in his photos, but they can't be the originals because he lost both on the battlefield.

That's Matthew Brady sitting on the lower step of the stairs on the right. Presumably that's Burn's wife, Barbara, standing next to him. She looks to be more than a match for Mr. Burns.

Originals

3A

3B

3C

3D

3E

3F

4 Town Central

What Happened

The center of Gettysburg, then and now, is a busy location variously called a *square*, a *circle*, or a *diamond*. We'll call it a *square*.

At around 4pm on July 1st, 1863, the Confederates simultaneously broke the Union lines west and north of town, driving the Federals back through town toward Cemetery Hill.

Rivers of blue Federals from the north and west flowed through town, most of them passing through the town square, closely followed by exhausted but jubilant Con-federates. But not all the Federals made it to Cemetery Hill. Many of them fled down alleys and side streets, and for the next two days Confederates captured hundreds of Union soldiers hiding in cellars, chicken coops, and under porches.

In any case, about 4:30pm, a South Carolina regiment planted its flag on the middle of the town square, and the Confederates would occupy the town for the remaining two days of battle.

Photo 4A   *Swan's Grocery on the Town Square* Photo taken in 1867 by C. J. Tyson. View looking W.

At the time of this photo in 1867, taken in the middle of the town square, the white building on the right was a grocery owned by John Swan. But at the time of the battle four years earlier, the grocery was owned and operated by Charles A. Boyer.

Mary McAllister, who lived on the same side of Chambersburg Street as Boyer's store (her house was across from Christ Lutheran Church seen in the background), noted that the "rebels were actually good to us. They went to Boyer's store at the corner and got canned fish and wanted us to cook them, and Martha did."

Austin C. Stearns of the 13th Massachusetts Infantry - a prisoner in Gettysburg during the Confederate occupation, wrote:

"I went up the street from Christ Lutheran Church to the Diamond to see and hear what was going on. As I was going along I saw a door open, and thought I would just look in and see how trade was, as it was a country grocery store (Boyer's). As I stepped in I saw it was in possession of half a dozen rebel soldiers, and they were having things all their own way. Some stood on the counter, others were behind, and all were busy; such things they wanted they laid aside in a pile and the others they gave a toss onto the floor. One of them looked up and said, "What does that damn Yank want?" Thinking my presence might not be agreeable to them, I turned to go out, when one of them gave one of their peculiar yells."

In 1885, the original structure was replaced by a more modern building.

Photo 4B   George Arnold's Store on the Town Square
View looking W down Chambersburg Street. Photo taken in early October 1863 by the Weaver Bros.

Here we're looking west in the same direction as Photo 4A, but looking at the opposite side of the street, four months after the battle. The first building to the left was the house and the clothing store of Gettysburg merchant, George Arnold, as well as a savings institution,

Desperately trying to stem the Confederate tide on the afternoon of July 1st, 1863, Union Battery I, 1st Ohio artillery, commanded by Capt. Hubert Dilger, set up shop in this square and blasted canister down Chambersburg Street in the direction of the camera view, as well as Carlisle Street running north (off to the right of the photo). The cannoneers' job was difficult because their own fleeing infantry was often in the way. Eventually Dilger's battery had to retreat, and around 4:30pm the 1st South Carolina regiment planted its battered flag here in the square.

On the early morning of July 4, 1863, after three day's of brutal fighting, Mr. Arnold saddled a horse and rode over Cemetery Hill, "with his white hair contrasting strangely with the rosiness of his cheeks." By chance, coming upon General Meade on Taneytown Road, just south of the future site of the Soldiers Cemetery. Arnold surprised the general by informing him that Ewell's Corps had just evacuated Gettysburg. Meade warmly thanked Mr. Arnold for the news.

The sixth building on the left in the photo - today 24 Chambersburg Street - the dark two-story brick building barely visible as it's sandwiched between two bigger buildings that look similar to each other, was the home of Robert McCurdy, the president of Gettysburg railroad. In this building after the battle, McCurdy cared for wounded Confederate Maj. Gen. Isaac R. Trimble, who had led one of the three divisions in Pickett's Charge, losing a leg in the process.

That cupola you see at the far end of the street belongs to the Christ Lutheran Church, which is still there today. During the Union retreat through town a chaplain, Capt. Horatio S. Howell of the 90th Pennsylvania infantry, was killed as he emerged from the church after caring for wounded soldiers inside. A monument on the bottom step of the church entrance now marks the incident. Sgt. Archibald Snow later described what happened:

"I had just had my wound dressed and was leaving through the front door just behind Chaplain Howell, at the same time when the advance skirmishers of the Confederates were coming up the street on a run. Howell, in addition to his shoulder straps & uniform, wore the straight dress sword prescribed in Army Regulations for chaplains. The first skirmisher arrived at the foot of the church steps just as the chaplain and I came out. Placing one foot on the first step the soldier called on the chaplain to surrender; but Howell, instead of throwing up his hands promptly and uttering the usual 'I surrender,' attempted some dignified explanation to the effect that he was a noncombatant and as such was exempt from capture, when a shot from the skirmisher's rifle ended the controversy. The man who fired the shot stood on the exact spot where the memorial tablet has since been erected, and Chaplain Howell, fell upon the landing at the top of the steps."

Rev. Capt. Horatio S. Howell

Photo 4C *Looking down Baltimore St. from the Town Square*

Photo taken around early October 1863 by P. S. Weaver. View looking south.

This photo, also taken from the town square four months after the battle, looks south down Baltimore Street. The building on the right, situated on the southeast corner of Gettysburg square in 1863, was known for obvious reasons as the "Schick Building." It was a dry goods store, but only on the bottom floor. The upper floors were the residence of the building owner, Prof. Martin Luther Stoever of Pennsylvania College. His daughter wrote in 1903 that the family's dining room served as a shelter for 20 Union soldiers wounded during the first day's fighting. Other Federals hid in the basement until the night of July 3rd, when they were discovered by the Confederates just as the battle ended. The next morning, July 4th, after the Confederates de-

parted, Union sharpshooters occupied portions of the building as it was one of the tallest in the town.

The large building with the steeple was and is the Gettysburg courthouse, built in 1859. The building served as both a hospital and observatory during the battle. Union Col. Henry A. Morrow of the 24th Michigan, wounded on July 1st and being held in town as a prisoner, later wrote that, from that cupola, he watched all the famous attacks made by the Confederates on the left, right, and center of the Union position over the following two days.

Hidden from view by shade trees planted along Baltimore Street in 1856, is the Fahnestock Brothers store (see Photo 4E) located at the far end of this block and just up from the courthouse.

Photo 4D   Looking South Down Baltimore Street from Town Square
Photo taken in 1889 by Mumper.   View looking south. Photo owned by William Frassantino.

This photo, also taken from the town square, looks south down Baltimore Street as does Photo 4C. This road leads to Evergreen Cemetery, and also to the Emmitsburg Road, which runs past Cemetery Ridge.

Both of the closest buildings in the photo, which still stand today, were dry goods stores at the time the photo was taken The one on the right was owned, but not operated, by Mr. John L. Schick. His three-story building was one of the tallest in Gettysburg at the time of the battle. Both buildings were commandeered by the U.S. Army for relief efforts immediately after the battle.

At the time of the photo, the building on the left was a business owned and operated by G. W. Spangler, but at the time of the battle, it was a house was owned by David and Catherine Wills. It was among the largest houses in town and on the evening of November 18, 1863 it overflowed with 38 dinner guests, including Abraham Lincoln. Mrs. Wills prepared several bedrooms for overnight guests, giving Lincoln their bedroom, where he polished the Gettysburg Address before the National Cemetery's dedication the next day.

That's snow on the road.

Photo 4E *Fahnestock Bros. Store on Baltimore Street*

Photo taken around July 9, 1863 by Gardner.   View looking NW.

Here we're looking at the Fahnestock store, a dry goods and clothing store. Union Maj. Gen. Oliver O. Howard, commander of the XI Corps and for a brief time, commander of the entire Union army at Gettysburg, used the roof in the rear portion of this building to observe the battlefield on July 1, 1863; but the structure proved too low for him to see westward beyond Seminary Ridge. Just to the left of this photo sat (and still sits) the taller cupola of the Adams County Court House (visible in Photo 4C). But at the time the door to the courthouse cupola was locked. While Howard's staff debated whether they should break down the door, Fahnestock's young son, delighted with all the excitement, walked over and volunteered the Fahnestock roof, which Howard accepted.

It was while Howard was on this roof that a rider called up from the street to notify him that General Reynolds had been killed, making Howard the senior Union commander on the field.

A military career seems an odd choice for Howard - a small, deeply religious man. He was brave enough, having lost his right arm in the battle of Fair Oaks a year earlier. He didn't approve of drinking and discouraged or prohibited it in his corps, which didn't go over well with his hard-drinking troops, especially his heavily German, beer-swilling troops. But he was always polite.

Once, hearing a teamster swearing a blue-streak, he called the man over to the side where he quietly admonished the bemused mule-driver not to use that kind of language again.

An ardent abolitionist, Howard later founded Howard University as a school for former slaves.

Two days after the battle, on the morning of July 6th, the U.S. Sanitary Commission commandeered the Fahnestock store, after which, as seen in this photo, "Carload after car load of supplies were brought to this place ... till the sidewalk was monopolized, and even the street encroached upon."

The front of the building has been greatly modified over the decades and doesn't look much like it did in 1863, but the basic structure of the old building is still there, underneath the facade.

Maj. Gen. Oliver O. Howard

Photo 4F   South Stratton Street looking toward German Reformed Church

Photo taken 1867 by C. J. Tyson.   View looking south.

No, this is not a sad example of war's destruction; this is what Gettysburg streets looked like on a *good* day! This slightly odd photo was taken four years after the battle. It's unclear if the man on the horse is the subject, or the condition of the street.

You're looking south down Stratton Street, which intersects with E. Middle Street where you see the man on the horse. After their line collapsed north of town, many soldiers of the Federal XI Corps fled down this street on their way to Cemetery Hill.

That's the German Reformed Church steeple on the right.

That prominent house you see on the far left of the photo, at 101 E. Middle Street, is still there today. At the time of the battle a Mr. Robert D. Armor lived there; he was a silversmith who also moonlighted as a janitor at the nearby public school.

This condition of this fairly well maintained, in-town street gives you just a faint idea of what the country roads must have been like when armies of thousands of troops, cavalry, artillery, and supply wagons passed over them, creating either muddy swamps or clouds of choking dust.

Photo 4G   St. James Lutheran Church on York & Stratton Streets

Photo taken in 1867 by C. J. Tyson. View looking south down Stratton Street.

Back in 1863, the church you see here, the St. James Lutheran Church at the corner of York and Stratton, a block east from the town square, was ministered by Rev. Abraham Essick. On the first day of fighting, the pastor stood for hours in the cupola of his church where he had a splendid view of the battle. But eventually, as Federal troops flooded past his church on their retreat down Stratton Street toward Cemetery Hill, the view became a bit too splendid when Confederate bullets started chipping the woodwork around the minister, forcing him back inside.

By the second day, the reverend decided it was time to leave since the Rebels "were getting very saucay [sic]." So he and a local college professor, Frederick Muhlenberg, struck out on foot for York Springs (called Petersburg at that time) about 14 miles away. According to the minister, "They passed through about 15,000 Rebel cavalry and they were tormented by them in every conceivable way. They even demanded the shoes from off our feet, which we only saved by appealing to the high officers."

The original church was torn down and rebuilt in 1912. Like all churches in town, it served as a hospital during and after the battle.

Note that white fence in the photo, just across the street from the church. Today it's a parking garage, but at the time of the battle that fence enclosed the front yard of Judge Samuel R. Russell's house.

A few days after the battle a Union body was discovered inside the fence. The dead soldier was Sgt. Amos Humiston of the 154th New York. He was fleeing with his XI Corps comrades down Stratton Street. Wounded either in the fighting north of town, or here on the street, he crawled into Russell's yard and died. When he was found, he was clutching his children's photo. Initially, no one could identify him, but after the children's photo was widely circulated in Northern newspapers, his widow eventually recognized them, and so identified its owner as her missing husband.

Sgt. Amos Humiston

This photo was found clutched in his hand. They're his children, from left, Franklin, Frederick and Alice.

4A

4B

4C

4D

4E

4F

4G

5 South Gettysburg

What Happened

As the Union forces west and north of town were driven back through Gettysburg's central square, a herd instinct propelled them toward Cemetery Hill. By late afternoon, a river of thousands of men walked, ran, and hobbled down Baltimore Street toward the cemetery on the southeast edge of town.

Fortunately for the Union, Maj. Gen. Oliver Howard had been expecting them, and he had been carefully stocking the hill with fresh infantry and artillery. So, although they were hanging on by their nails, the Federals' rout more or less ended as they reached the top of the hill and turned to face their pursuers. The irony, completely lost on them at the moment, was that they had been driven back to the "good ground" where Buford and later Howard had wanted them to be in the first place.

Facing the one-armed Howard was the one-legged Confederate corps commander on the scene, Lt. Gen. Richard Ewell (known as "Old Baldhead" by his troops). It was growing dark, and his formations were in disarray from their earlier fighting, scattered and chasing Yankees around town. The hill appeared to be packed with Yankee artillery. Also he had orders from Lee "not to bring on a major engagement," though in fact he was already in a major engagement.

Ewell decided to halt the attack for the night.

His decision seemed obvious to him at the time, and he made it without much hesitation. None of his subordinate commanders seriously disagreed. But he would later be harshly criticized in the South for halting the pursuit. He had just taken over command of Stonewall Jackson's corps after that demi-god's death two months earlier, and Southerners were convinced that "Old Jack" would have never stopped when he had the Yankees on the run, and they were probably right - for better or worse.

In any case, the front lines of the two armies now faced each other at this southeastern end of town, and though there would be no major attacks here for the remainder of the battle, the houses and buildings on this front line would be used for constant skirmishing and sharpshooting throughout the next two days of battle, In effect, the fighting here would be house to house - a rarity in the Civil War.

Lt. Gen. Richard S. Ewell

Photo 5A   The Battlefield Hotel (Wagon Hotel) at Baltimore St. and Emmitsburg Road

View looking South.   Photo taken in July 1886 by an unknown photographer.

In this photo, taken two decades after the battle, we're looking south toward what was at the time of the battle the Wagon Hotel.

On July 2nd and 3rd, this intersection was a front line between the two armies. Constant sniper fire made the street extremely dangerous, with Federals in the hotel firing toward the camera, while Confederates answered from buildings on the left and right of this camera position.

Across from the hotel just off camera to the left, sits the McClellan house, where a Confederate bullet penetrated the side door and made one of its occupants - Miss Jennie Wade - famous as the only civilian killed in the battle.

Soon after the war, with an eye on the booming tourist trade, the hotel's name was changed to the *Battlefield Hotel*. The building burned down in 1895. It's now a busy convenience store. Baltimore Street on the left continues its route up to Cemetery Hill about a half mile away. The street to the right merges with Emmitsburg Road about a mile south, and eventually cuts across the entire front of Cemetery Ridge, where the 3rd day's climatic battle was fought.

During the occupation, hiding indoors at her family home on Baltimore Street near the edge of the Rebel-controlled area, Anna Garlach watched as a deadly game was played out across the street. "The [Weinbrenner] building along the alley was brick and the men there formed a kind of barricade on the pavement," she later noted. From my protected position, some of the Rebels "put a hat on a stick over the barricade [to] ... draw the fire of the Union sharpshooters." Whenever a Yankee riflemen on nearby Cemetery Hill took the bait, other Confederates hiding nearby would "jump up and fire from the street."

The Federals did the same thing, shooting in pairs, the first shot causing the enemy snipers to duck, and the second, coming right after the first, catching them as they bobbed up to retaliate. This was *Sniper Ruse #1*. Both sides soon countered with *Ruse #2*, which involved faking a quick return, causing the second shooter to miss. So now they had to devise a way to defeat *Ruse #2*, so they came up with *Ruse #3*, where the shooters began operating in teams of three, with the third man delaying his shot long enough to let the enemy believe he had managed to dodge the whole series. And there probably would have been a *Ruse #4* and *#5* if the battle hadn't ended in just three days.

It was indeed a dangerous game, but quite exciting. One New Jersey sniper later reflected, "Alas!" "How little we thought human life was the stake for which this game was being played."

Photo 5B Looking N up Baltimore St. toward the Battlefield Hotel (Wagon Hotel)

View looking N. Photo taken by Gardner in July 1865.

This photo, taken two years after the battle, gives us another view of the Wagon Hotel on the left, but this time from the Union side, looking northwest down Baltimore Street toward the center of town. Baltimore Street breaks sharply toward the camera, on its way up Cemetery Hill, less than half a mile behind the camera.

Between the hotel and that little white house next to it runs what was then Emmitsburg Road (today Steinwehr Avenue). Just beyond that white house sat the residence and cannery of John Rupp, evidenced by the smoke stack. Rupp's area was occupied by Confederates, and became a Confederate snipers' nest.

To the far right in the photograph, closest to the camera on the right, sat the white, two-story residence of Catherine Snyder. Hidden next to the Snyder house in those trees was McClellan house, where Jennie Wade was famously killed. There's still some damage, presumably from the battle, on the side of the Synder house.

On the late afternoon of July 1st, 1863, thousands of Union troops of the I Corps and XI Corps streamed down Baltimore Pike from town, heading toward the camera and onward to Cemetery Hill, with the Confederates on their tail. The Federal frontline became the hotel, while the Confederates faced them from Rupp's cannery. From these locations the two sides fought deadly sniper battles throughout the remainder of the battle, And there were sniper duels elsewhere around the battlefield, not just here in town.

(Actually, they weren't called snipers back then; they were called *sharpshooters*).

.

Photo 5C   *Procession to dedicate the National Cemetery*
View looking N to the intersection of Baltimore St and Emmitsburg Road (Steinwher Ave today).
Photo taken November 19, 1863 by an unknown photographer.

In this view, taken five months after the battle, we're facing in the same direction as in Photo 5B - looking north and slightly west down Baltimore Street - but closer to the intersection, and it gives us a view of the procession dedicating the National Soldiers' Cemetery on November 19, 1963. The photographer caught the procession just as it was about to turn right (left in the photo) on what was then Emmitsburg Road (today Steinwehr Avenue). No doubt there was a band playing.

The Wagon Hotel sits just off camera to the left; it served, as already discussed, as the Union front line in the town during the second two day's fighting.

Within a month of the battle, plans were made to construct a cemetery - a national cemetery - and collect the bodies of all the Union soldiers hastily buried around the battlefield. A 17 acre plot was selected on the summit of Cemetery Hill, just west of then-existing civilian graveyard, Evergreen Cemetery.

On October 27, 1863, the Federal government began the grisly task of removing all Union dead from their makeshift graves, which were scattered for miles around the battlefield. The job took months, and was very much still in progress when the cemetery's formal dedication took place on November 19th. By then a few hundred bodies had already been disinterred from the battlefield and reburied in the cemetery.

Though not visible in the photo, Abraham Lincoln must be somewhere in the front of the procession, on his way to the cemetery to deliver his famed Gettysburg Address.

Photo 5D *South Washington St. looking toward Town.*
View looking N. Photo taken in July 1886 by an unknown photographer.

When the 9,000 troops of the Union XI Corps reached Gettysburg near noon on July 1st, 1863, they heard the sounds of battle rumbling through the town streets. The thunder came from the west, where the Union I Corps was already heavily engaged.

One of the XI Corps' divisions, Barlow's, hurriedly marched up this street, Washington Street, to the cheers of Gettysburg residents. The troops were winded and the weather muggy. Women stood on the sidewalks with pails and ladles, allowing soldiers to grab a quick gulp of water without breaking formation.

The troops were heading to a position north of town and, as it turned out, to disaster. The XI Corps already had a rotten reputation in the Union army and it certainly wouldn't improve at Gettysburg. The corps' insignia was a half-moon, and the other soldiers derisively called it the "Flying Crescent" because the corps was

routed just two month's earlier at Chancellorsville by Stonewall Jackson. Although in fact, the corps was left in an exposed position in that battle, where a rout was almost inevitable. The other problem was that about half the units in the XI Corps were German immigrants, called "Dutch," who couldn't speak much English and who had impossibly long names. Germans and Irish were low on American society's totem pole at the time, but at least the Irish could speak English, sort of.

This photo, commissioned by Union veterans 23 years after the battle, was probably taken because the street looked much the same to them in 1886 as it did in 1863. And in fact, it looks pretty much today like it did in 1886. Many of the same houses still stand today.

Photo 5E   McClellan House where Jennie Wade was killed
View looking SE across Baltimore St.   Photo taken around 1865 by the Tyson Bros.

This is the house where 20-year-old Jennie Wade was killed, making her famous as the only civilian killed in the battle. She was at the house assisting her sister, Mrs. McClellan and her three-day-old baby. On the morning the third day of fighting, Jenny was struck by a sniper's bullet ploughing through that door on the left side of the house, which is barely visible in the photo. From its location, the shot had to have come from the Confederate side.

The photo was taken at least one or two years after the battle. It's unclear if the damaged fence is a result of the battle. Today, a hotel jams up next to the house. But the house, and (supposedly) the same door with its single, pristine bullet hole, remains a popular tourist attraction. In fact, the house had well over a hundred bullet marks after the battle, most of them presumably aimed at doors and windows.

Jennie Wade

Jennie Wade's actual nickname was "Ginnie," but history has decided it's "Jennie," and so we'll go along with that here as well.

On July 1st, 1863, the first day of fighting at Gettysburg, Jennie, her mother, and two younger brothers left their home in central Gettysburg and walked to the house of her sister, Georgia Anna Wade McClellan, at 528 Baltimore Street to assist her and her newborn child.

At the end of the first day's fighting, the house sat in no-man's-land with lead whizzing back and forth outside in the street.

More than 150 bullets struck the McClellan house during the fighting., but around 8:30am on July 3rd, with 160,000 men blasting away at each other all over Gettysburg, including in the street right outside the house, Jennie got to thinking what you're probably thinking: this would be a perfect time to bake biscuits. While she bustled about the kitchen and rolled out the dough, a bullet, fired from the Confederate position, penetrated the outside door, and then an inner kitchen door - which may or may not have been closed - striking Jennie in the back and piercing her heart before finally stopping in her corset. She died without a sound.

It seems odd that a sniper would waste a shot at a house where there had never been any Federal counter-fire, and quite a coincidence that the bullet went precisely in her direction. Baking in the 1800s had to be a noisy process, involving banging around metal pans, metal utensils, and iron stove doors, plus slamming dough on a table. There was a lull in the fighting on Culps Hill, so the street was probably quiet. We don't know where the sniper was; he might have been right outside the door. The kitchen racket may have attracted his attention, and he shot at the noise, not just the door.

We'll never know for sure.

On July 4th, Jennie's mother baked 15 loaves of bread with the dough Jennie had rolled out, and distributed most of it to the soldiers.

Jenny's grave, marked by a statue, is located in Evergreen Cemetery.

Jennie's Family

There's no reports of Jennie walking the wild side - she was in fact an active member of the St. James Lutheran Church (Photo 4G). But her family's reputation around town was rougher than a cob.

For openers, Jennie's brother-in-law, John Louis McClellan, joined the 21st Pennsylvania Cavalry in February 1864 but deserted. But above all there was Jennie's father, James Wade, a tailor, reputed to be the most dangerous dressmaker in Gettysburg. He definitely had some rough edges; he was arrested the year before he married Jennie's mother in 1840, and charged in Adams County Court that he "with force and arms, etc. Did commit fornication with a certain Mary Kuhn, single woman, and a male bastard child on the body of her, said Mary Kuhn, give them beget .." Though James Wade beat the rap, the resulting child, James A. Wade Jr. (born in early 1839), was reared as Jennie's older brother.

Jennie Wade on the right, her sister Georgia Anna on the left, and a family friend, Mary Comfort, in the center.

In May 1841 a tavern-keeper accused James of setting his stable on fire. That charge was dropped, but in 1842 he was arrested again, this time for assault and battery. Found guilty, he spent two weeks in county jail. The next year, in 1843, he was again charged with assault and battery, but the charges were dropped. In 1850, he was found guilty of - guess what - assault and battery, but he was only required to pay fine of one dollar plus court costs.

Remember, this was all happening in a town of 2,400 people. It looked like the law couldn't or wouldn't handle him. He probably scared more than a few of Gettysburg residents.

Then later in the same year, he was indicted on a felony charge of larceny. This time he was convicted and sentenced to two years of solitary confinement in the state penitentiary.

By 1852, James had done his time and was expecting to be released. But, possibly with some encouragement from the town's vigilante committee, his wife (Jennie's mother, Mary Ann) had James declared insane and committed to the Adams County Alms House in Gettysburg, where he was confined for the next 20 years until his death in 1872.

In 1855, Mary Ann had another child, Harry M. Wade, which was particularly remarkable since by that time her husband James, and presumably his

sperm, had been locked up across town in the insane asylum for three years.

Mary Ann's side of the family had a few legal blemishes of its own: In 1856, Thaddeus Filby, Mary Anne's younger brother and Jennie's uncle, was accused of larceny. That charge was dropped. But in 1862 he was found guilty of assault and battery on his wife, Harriet, and sentenced to three months in county jail. He enlisted in Company M, 21st Pennsylvania Cavalry in early 1864, and died a year later from wounds he received in action at Petersburg, Virginia.

In January 1866, an author wrote to the then famous John Burns for information concerning Jennie Wade. The cantankerous Burns, jealous of Jennie's posthumous fame, responded by dismissing Miss Wade as a "she-rebel," telling the author "the less said about her the better." Burns was not the only one in town who resented Jennie's posthumous fame.

The" Romance"

Jennie Wade, Jack Skelly and Wesley Culp were childhood friends, all raised in Gettysburg. They seemed to weave in and out of each other's lives like characters in a Russian novel. Within 10 days after the battle they would all be dead.

Wesley Culp joined the Confederate army the same day his brother and Jack Skelly enlisted with the Union. Two weeks before the battle of Gettysburg, as the Confederate army marched north. Culp's and Skelly's units clashed at Winchester, Virginia. After the battle, Culp found Skelly, who had been wounded. Skelly gave Culp a message to be delivered to Skelly's mother should Culp find himself in Gettysburg.

Although Culp's unit did in fact fight at Gettysburg, and although he did get a chance to briefly visit his sister in the town on the evening of July 1, he never had the opportunity to deliver the message to Skelly's mother. Culp was killed the next morning near Culp's Hill. Jenny Wade, who would never learn of Skelly's wounding, was killed on July 3rd. Skelly died of his wounds at Winchester on July 12, 1863, never knowing of Jennie's and Culp's deaths.

For the last century or so, Gettysburg tour guides and merchants have titillated tourist-romantics with the possibility that Jennie and Skelly were lovers, maybe even secretly married. But that scenario is stoutly refuted by the descendents of the Skelly family, who apparently did not then and do not now approve of Jennie or her family. No letters from Jack Skelly to Jennie Wade are known to exist. The one letter existing from Jennie Wade to Jack Skelly suggests that the two were good friends, but not necessarily lovers. It was written just six months before Jennie's death, while Jack Skelly's unit was stationed at Winchester Virginia, and signed "May I ever remain your true friend and well-wisher."

Wesley Culp - Killed on or near Culp's Hill

John Wesley Culp is remembered as the Southern soldier who fought and died on his family property during the battle. As discussed, he was also good friends with two other Gettysburg residents, Jennie Wade and Jack Skelly. But Culp actually only lived in Gettysburg from 1848 through 1856, the middle years of his short life. At age 21, he joined the 2nd Virginia Infantry, Co. B., at Harpers Ferry on April 20, 1861 which, as already mentioned, turned out to be the same day that his brother, William Culp, and his friend Jack Skelly, signed up with the 2nd Pennsylvania Infantry for three months service.

The units of Culp and Skelly soon clashed at Martinsburg, Virginia, with the Confederates being surprised and routed. Skelly wrote home that "If we had been 15 minutes sooner we might have had a chance [to capture them]. We found their knapsacks and blankets and have their canteens. They left everything they couldn't get off. Wes Culp was among them. He was seen by some of the citizens of Martinsburg..."

In June of 1862 Wesley Culp was captured at the Battle of Winchester and forced to take the oath of allegiance to the United States to obtain his freedom. Upon his release he immediately joined a band of guerrillas but was promptly captured again. He was again exchanged on August 5, 1862, presumably again swearing allegiance to the U.S., whereupon he promptly rejoined his Virginia regiment.

In June of 1863, as part of Lee's army advance north, Culp's regiment again clashed with his brother's and Jack Skelly's Pennsylvania regiment near Winchester, Virginia. This time it was the Yankees who were on the run. Culp wrote home that he heard that "Brother William was at Winchester but I didn't see him. He and the rest of [the] Yanks ran too fast."

Jack Skelly was wounded in this action. Somehow Culp found him and promised to deliver a letter from Jack to his (Skelly's) mother in Gettysburg, should Wesley be in that area.

By July 1, 1863, Culp's regiment was definitely in that area. His unit was part of the Stonewall brigade, positioned on the eastern side of the Confederate perimeter near Culp's Hill, a property owned by his father's first cousin, Henry Culp. On the evening of the first day's fighting, the Confederates occupied most of the town of Gettysburg. Wesley wanted to visit his family and submitted a request to the brigade commander, Brig. Gen. James Walker ("Stonewall Jim"). Delighted to have a Marylander fighting for the Southern cause, Walker agreed to see him and gave him a pass.

And so an elated Wesley started at once for town, just one or two miles away. He only had time for a hasty visit and, probably thinking he would have a chance to do so later, he didn't deliver Skelly's letter to his mother. He returned to his unit late that night and went on the skirmish line with his company early the next morning, where he was killed in a skirmish with the 28th Pennsylvania.

Apparently in response to an inquiry from Culp's family trying to locate his body, a Confederate soldier responded, "Yes, Wes Culp was a little fellow, very boyish looking. I think he was about 22 years old when he was killed.... He was killed instantly, shot through the head.... He was killed in advance of our skirmish line."

Ironically, in a battle where 30% - 40% regimental casualty rates were the norm, Wesley Culp was the only member of his 2nd Virginia regiment to be killed in the battle, although two of the regiment later died of wounds. Culp was buried and his grave supposedly marked by comrades in his regiment. But though his family diligently searched for his grave, the only remains they ever found was a rifle stock with his name carved on it.

The story goes that he was killed on Culp's Hill, his family's ancestral land. Actually, that's probably not exactly true, although close.

The skirmish occurred near the Hanover Road and on the extreme left of the 2nd Virginia's line on the Culp's land. However, it appears likely that the 2nd Virginia skirmishers had already crossed Culp's property and forded the eastern side of Rock Creek by dawn. So it seems doubtful that Wesley was actually killed the farm of his father's first cousin, Henry Culp. But he did die on property adjacent to his family's ancestral land, and he must have known that whole area very well.

In fact, it was probably his knowlege of the area that got him killed. As his Confederate comrade later wrote, Culp was out in *front* of his skirmish line when he was killed, which was a very dangerous place to be. Likely he was out there because he knew the area, and he walked up on a Federal skirmish line, close enough to be shot in the head instead of the chest, all of which may explain why he was the one of the few fatalities in his regiment that day.

Jack Skelly

Both of these photos are owned by the Gettysburg National Park.

John Wesley Culp

5A

5B

5C

5D

5E

6 Little Round Top

What Happened

By the morning of July 2nd, the Union army occupied a formable defensive position along the heights of Cemetery Ridge. Lee should have taken one look at that ridge and realized it was suicide to attack the Yankees there. His best corps commander, Lt. Gen. James Longstreet, urged him to forget Gettysburg and swing the entire army south around the Union line and feint toward Washington or Philadelphia, forcing the Federals to fight Lee on ground of his own choosing. But Lee wouldn't listen. He was determined to fight here, destroy the Union army, and finish this awful war here and now.

But Lee and the Confederates had a secret weapon: Union General Daniel Sickles. The left flank of the Federal line on Cemetery Ridge was supposed to be anchored on Little Round Top. Gen. George Meade, Union army commander for exactly five days, ordered his III Corps commander, Maj. Gen. Dan Sickles, to occupy the hill. For various reasons, Sickles didn't. Instead of occupying Little Round Top, Sickles deployed some of his men directly in *front* of the hill, on Devil's Den and its adjoining ridge, Houck's Ridge. Worse, he then stretched out the remainder of his troops on a defensive line running all the way to Emmitsburg Road, a half mile or so to the west. It was way too much real estate for one corps to defend, and his corps was "in the air" - unsupported on its flanks.

On the second day of the battle, Lee planned to hit the entire Union line with a "wave" attack, striking first at the south end of the line at Little Round Top, then the Wheatfield, then the Peach Orchard, etc., all the way north to Cemetery Hill and Culps Hill.

Lee ordered Longstreet to launch the attack beginning around noon at the latest. But for various reasons, possibly including Longstreet's reluctance, the Confederates didn't attack until 3:30pm or 4pm. Confederate division commander Maj. Gen. John Bell Hood got the assignment to take Little Round Top. Hood's men launched their assault from almost a mile away, from a height called Warfield Ridge, an extension of the south end of Seminary Ridge.

When the Confederate attack began and Meade heard peppering fire from Little Round Top, he dispatched one of his aides, Brig. Gen. Gouverneur Warren to "yonder hill" to see what it was about.

When Warren reached the hill's summit, he was horrified to discover it was unoccupied except for a few army signalers while, looking to his southwest, a Confederate battleline advanced toward him. Warren frantically dispatched messengers in every direction, calling for help. Various Federal units near the base of Little Round Top responded. They raced up the hill from the north, while Confederates advanced up the hill from the south and west. The Federals won the race to the summit, though just barely.

From then until dark, the Federals repelled attack after attack, always managing to plug gaps in their line at the last minute. By the end of the day the Federals had been pushed off Devil's Den and Houck's Ridge, but they still clung to Little Round Top. The following day, July 3rd, Lee assaulted the center of the Union line, and there was little fighting here on the Round Tops as both sides entrenched themselves behind the abundant supply of rocks in this area.

Modern panorama taken from Little Round Top looking west. Devil's Den is on the left, Houck's Ridge is in the center, and behind the ridge is Rose's Woods. Just behind the right side of that tree line is the Wheatfield. That far distant treeline is Seminary Ridge, where Lee launched attacks on both July 2nd and 3rd.

Photo 6A   *Looking W from summit of Little Round Top toward Houcks Ridge*
Photo taken by Brady & Co. around July 15, 1863.

This photo, taken about ten days after the battle, is the first known to be taken from the summit of Little Round Top. Here we're looking west and a bit north. The Confederates attacked toward the camera position from both the front and from the left. That tree line in the far distance is Seminary Ridge, the launching point of the Confederate attacks.

You can see a portion of Devil's Den on the left side of the photo. It was from the top of Devil's Den that Union Capt. James Smith of the 4th NY Light Artillery, positioned four of his six guns, opening a devastating fire on the advancing Confederates. Among many other casualties was Confederate division commander John Bell Hood, whose arm was nearly ripped off by a shell fragment.

That rise with all the rocks directly across from Little Round Top is Houcks Ridge. The valley directly below the ridge is Plum Run Valley (or more dramatically, *The Valley of Death* - a name given it by the news media of the time.) Plum Run is a creek that runs through the valley. In 1863, both the ridge and the valley were owned by John Houck, an elderly farmer who lived in town at what is today 218 Baltimore Street, near the Presbyterian Church.

Brig. Gen. J. Hobart Ward commanded the Federal brigade that held this ridge as the left flank of the Union army; his troops lined up along its summit, with their backs to the camera.

While Confederates attacked Little Round Top from camera-left, they also attacked Houcks Ridge directly from the front until they finally cracked the Federal line, sending the survivors fleeing up here to Little Round Top.

The tree line on the opposite side of the ridge marks the line between Houck's property and that of John Rose. The trees are part of 70 acre Rose Woods, which was occupied by the Confederate forces as they advanced through that timber to attack not only Houcks Ridge but also the Wheatfield, which is out of camera view to the right. For much of the afternoon of July 2nd, 1863, someone standing here would have seen the entire area from left to right ablaze with battle.

Confederate General Longstreet ordered an attack that struck in consecutive waves stretching from Little Round Top, Devil's Den, the Wheatfield, the Peach Orchard, and then on up Emmitsburg Road. The 1st Texas and 3rd Arkansas advanced on the left side of this photo, heading in this direction. The Texans continued in this direction to strike Devils Dan, while the Arkansas troops entered Rose Woods. Not long thereafter, portions of the Brig. Gens. Henry Benning's and George Anderson's Georgia brigades also advanced in this direction, on their way to strike Houcks Ridge.

The buildings in the left-center of the distant treeline of the photo were part of the farm owned in 1863 by Philip Snyder, located on Emmitsburg Road on the southern end of Seminary Ridge, The Snyder barn can be seen to the immediate right of his house in the photo. The woods behind the farm were owned by J. Biesecker. It was from those woods that the Confederate brigades of Robertson, Benning, and Anderson emerged in battleline formation, advancing in this direction. Soon thereafter, two more Confederate brigades commanded by Brig. Gens. Joseph Kershaw and Paul Semmes stepped off from the same woods, but to the right of the Snyder farm.

The photograph was taken from along the highest ground on the summit of Little Round Top, several yards east of where the monument of the 91st Pennsylvania infantry stands today.

There are two people in the period photo - the one with his back to the camera is an assistant; the other, perfectly camouflaged in the shadows, is seated at the lower right and facing right. He's probably Matthew Brady, who wore that type of straw hat - called a skimmer.

And though they're hard to see - just tiny dots without magnification - Frassantino spotted cattle peacefully grazing in the Plum Run creek in the photo - the site of such savage fighting less than two weeks earlier; they're just above those three flat rocks behind Brady's head.

Photo 6B   View looking up at the Round Tops
View looking SE. Photo taken by Brady & Co. around July 15, 1863.

Here's the opposite view of Photo 6A, looking east, up at Little Round Top and Big Round Top. The place looks perfectly normal, considering a bloody battle was fought here just 10 days earlier.

Recorded from a camera position near the northeastern edge of the Wheatfield, Brady's photograph shows both Little Round Top (left) and Big Round Top (right). Brady himself is on the far left, gazing across the marshy flatland of Plum Run Valley.

Note the difference between the two hills. Over the years, farmers cut down the trees on Little Round Top for lumber or firewood, making it easy to see Confederate movements coming from the west; whereas Big Round Top is tree-covered. That's why Little Round Top played a much more prominent role in the battle than did it's big brother.

Photo 6C Looking NW from summit of Little Round Top
Photo taken by Mumper in 1889. View looking NW. Photo owned by William Frassantino.

This tremendous view from the summit of Little Round Top, taken a quarter century after the battle, looks more to the right (northwest) than does Photo 6A. In this photo you can easily see Seminary Ridge - that far tree line on this side of the distant hills. It was from Seminary Ride that that Lee launched assaults on July 2nd and July 3rd.

The main Union line on Cemetery Ridge was off camera to the right, as is Gettysburg.

The summit's western view here shows you why this hill was so valuable to the Union army. A rabbit couldn't cross those fields without the Federals spotting it, at least in the daytime. As discussed earlier, the Federals had this fine view because local farmers had cleared the trees on this western side of the hill.

However, it didn't work in reverse; had the Confederates occupied this hill - which they never did - they would not have enjoyed a similar view of the Union line, because much of the northern side of Little Round Top was tree covered. The summit is also covered with massive boulders, making it extremely difficult to haul up artillery and fire on the Union line in a northerly direction. And even had the Confederates managed to take the hill and haul a few cannons up, plus ammuni-

tion, fifty Union guns from numerous locations could easily have pulverized the entire hilltop. Moral: The infantry fight for Little Round Top was not quite as vital to Union victory as present day movies would have you believe!

Somewhere in that valley below is Plum Run Creek. The tree-covered rise on the left is the northern end of Houcks Ridge, held by the Federals on July 2nd before they were driven off and forced to flee here to Little Round Top. On the opposite side of Houcks Ridge, in that open area on the left, lies the Wheatfield. You can even see the Wheatfield monuments. The Wheatfield was the scene of ferocious fighting in the hours after Little Round Top was attacked. That's Wheatfield Road on the right.

Those trees on the left, on both sides of the Wheatfield, are part of Rose Woods. The Rose Farm sits out of sight on the far side of the Wheatfield, behind that second bank of trees. You'll see much more of the Rose Farm in Chapter 10.

Photo 6D   Looking NE from Little Round Top toward Cemetery Ridge

View looking toward Cemetery Hill and Ziegler's Grove. Photo taken by Brady & Co. around July 15, 1863.

This photo of distant Cemetery Ridge - the main Union line on July 2nd and 3rd - was taken less than two weeks after the battle, and it's the only one taken of the Ridge for decades thereafter. For some reason photographers of that era just didn't get the importance of Cemetery Ridge. Even in this photo, Brady chose to emphasize that big rock, blocking much of the view.

But still visible in the photo are Wheatfield Road (between the boulder and the large tree to the right); it was just a farm lane at the time. Also you can see the farm of George Weikert (to the immediate right and on level with the top of the boulder). The farm is still there today.

Ziegler's Grove, the right anchor of the Union line on Cemetery Ridge (left in the photo), is barely visible in the photo; and behind the Grove, some trees in Evergreen Cemetery can be seen. Most importantly, you can just make out the "Copse of Trees" which served as the central aiming point for the Confederate attack on the third day - it's on the same horizon line as Ziegler's Grove but about in the center of the treeline.

Photo 6E   Union Breastworks on South Slope of Little Round Top

View looking NW. Photo taken by Brady & Co. around July 15, 1863.

Here we see the top of the Little Round Top summit, as opposed to the other photos that focus on the surrounding view.

The photo was taken about 10 days after the battle and you can see the stone breastworks constructed by the Federals. During the actual fighting on July 2nd, the Federals had no fortifications. They only built them on the night of July 2nd, and the next day. But the hill was never attacked again after the afternoon of July 2nd.

This spot is easily found today, as a prominent statue of Gen. Warren now stands atop the boulder above that rail leaning against the pine tree.

This was the only photo in the collection where I could see clouds in the original. So I added some clouds to this color photo as well.

Photo 6F 44th New York Breastworks on Little Round Top
View looking S towards Big Round Top. Photo taken by Gibson around July 7th, 1863.

Taken four years apart, this view and Photo 6G depict the identical boulder in the foreground, which was probably part of the works of the 44th New York Regiment of Col. Vincent Strong's brigade.

The sticks leaning against the rocks were probably used as tent poles for ponchos, which were needed due to the rains following the battle.

The 44th New York fought off numerous attacks, especially by the 5th Texas, and also probably elements of the 4th Texas on camera-left and the 4th Alabama on camera-right. But during the fight, the Federals didn't have the benefit of these sturdy breastworks although they did still have these handy boulders for cover. They had just barely reached the top of the hill before colliding with the attacking Confederates. It was only after dark on July 2nd that they had time to construct these fortifications which, as it turned out, were not attacked again.

To the left of the 44th New York was the 83rd Pennsylvania, and to the left of the Pennsylvanians was the left flank of the Union line on Little Round Top, manned by the famous 20th Maine.

This location is easy to find - it's at the south end of Little Round Top just behind the "Castle Monument" (the 44th NY monument). The Park even has this same photo on display there.

Photo 6G Looking to Bushman Farm
View looking SW. Photo taken by the Weaver Bros. in 1867. Photo owned by Wm Frassantino

Taken four years after Photo 6F, this stereo photo shows the identical boulder in the foreground (or at least the right edge of it), but from a different vantage point.

That distant tree line, Warfield Ridge, marked the stepping-off point for Confederate Maj. Gen. John Bell Hood's division in its assault against this location on Little Round Top. As you can see, it was a pretty good walk, actually a trot, across the fields just to reach this point. And some of the Confederates had marched

nearly 25 miles that same day, before they even reached the battlefield.

Visible in the photo is the barn (left) and house (right) of Michael Bushman. The buildings still stand today. Brig. Gen. Jerome Robertson's Texas brigade advanced in line of battle toward this location from the right side of the photo, whereas Brig. Gen. Evander Law's Alabama brigade line advanced on the left of the photo. As you can see, much of that advance was across open fields, and therefore under heavy cannon fire from the four

Federal guns positioned on top of Devil's Den (out of sight below on camera-right).

Two of Law's regiments - the 47th and 15th Alabama - scrambled up Big Round Top to camera-left, where they got into a sharp fight with elements of the 2nd U.S. Sharpshooter's Regiment. After driving the pesky sharpshooters off Big Round Top, the two Alabama regiments advanced down this side of Big Round Top and one of them, the 15th Alabama, famously attacked the 20th Maine in fighting off to the left of this photo. The 47th Alabama attacked the troops of 83rd Pennsylvania, whose line was just to the left of the camera.

Nearly every Gettysburg guide for the last century has regaled tourists with the dramatic account about how General Warren, upon reaching the summit of the Little Round Top, ordered a cannon shot fired into the distant woods, and in doing so, he spotted a glint of a bayonet and realized to his horror that the Confederates were about to attack the hill.

It's a wonderful story.

Alas, this photo shows why the wonderful story has to be a myth. The Confederates didn't tip-toe up to Little Round Top. Instead, they lined up by the thousands and advanced across those open fields in full battle formation, flags flying, and probably with drums beating cadence, from almost a mile away. Their advance would have been abundantly apparent.

And there are other reasons the story has to be a myth:

1. There *were* no Federal cannon on Little Round Top when Warren arrived. In fact that was the whole prob-

lem. (Although there were Union four cannon, probably already firing, down below, atop Devil's Den).

2. By the time Warren reached the summit, 20 or 30 cannon of Longstreet's artillery already dueling with 20 or 30 cannon of the Federals in the Peach Orchard. Basically, cannons were blasting away all over the place by the time Warren reached Little Round Top, and it's unlikely one dinky cannon shot from this location would have rattled the Confederate line.

3. July 2nd, 1863 was a hazy, overcast day. There *was* no bright sun to glint on a Confederate bayonet. In any case, infantrymen usually didn't fix bayonets until they advanced out of the treeline to dress their ranks in the open field.

4. Last but not least, even with binoculars, could *you* see a bayonet glint inside those woods, through the smoke of an artillery shell that had just landed there? And how would you know it was a bayonet? And even if you could see it and knew it was a bayonet, so what? A glinting bayonet or even the fact that the woods were enemy occupied doesn't necessarily equal an imminent attack.

Anyway, The 4th and 5th Texas assaulted this position in front of the camera. One 4th Texan complained, "We had to fight the Yankees on a mountain!" Another from the 5th Texas said, "The balls [were] whizzing so thick it seemed like you could hold up a hat and catch it full."

6A

Originals

6B

6C

6D

6E

6F

6G

7 Devils Den

What Happened

Devils Den's massive boulders seem to have magically sprouted out of the ground, and only here; there's nothing like them anywhere else in the rock-covered Gettysburg area or possibly anywhere in the eastern U.S. The boulders might have attracted tourists today even if there had never been a battle.

It was only as the two sides clashed that the combatants first laid eyes on these rocks. Even in the roar of battle, they must have been amazed at the size of these boulders, probably thinking they had indeed entered the gates of hell.

As previously discussed, on the afternoon of July 2nd, Union Brig. Gen. J. Hobart Ward's brigade manned these boulders and the ridge directly behind it (photo-right) - Houcks Ridge. The boulders marked the southern anchor of his brigade and in fact the southern anchor of the entire Union army. His brigade was badly misplaced. It should have been safely anchored back here on top of Little Round Top. But Ward's III Corps commander, Maj. Gen. Dan Sickles, ordered Ward to this position, contrary to Sickle's orders from General Meade.

Atop the Devils Den boulders, Ward placed four cannon commanded by Capt. James Smith and his 4th New York Battery.

Around 3:30pm, Lt. Gen. James Longstreet launched wave after wave of Confederate brigades against the III Corps line. The first wave struck Little Round Top, and shortly after that the next wave attacked the Federal positions atop the boulders of Devil's Den.

In ferocious fighting that consumed not only Devil's Den, but the Triangular Field just to the west (a small field fenced with boulders in a triangular shape), and soon Ward's entire position on Houcks Ridge, Confederates eventually broke the Union line, forcing the survivors to flee to the safety of Little Round Top. The Confederates, however, failed to take Little Round Top and so by the evening of July 2nd, the two sides glared at each other across Plum Run Valley - with the Confederates holding Devil's Den and Houcks Ridge, and the Federals positioned here on the hill. The two sides sniped at each other throughout the following day, but the major combat ended here on the late afternoon of July 2nd.

Modern view of Devil's Den (on left) from Little Round Top. Houck's Ridge is directly to the right of Devil's Den, and that's Rose Woods behind Houck's Ridge. The Triangular Field adjoins Devil's Den, to the right of that big tree on the left.

Photo 7A   Dead Confederate "Sharpshooter" behind Devil Den wall.
View looking E toward the Round Tops. Photo taken by O'Sullivan around July 6th or 7th, 1863.

Here is one of the most famous photos of the Civil War - maybe *the* most famous. Gardner and his photographer, Timothy O'Sullivan, labeled the corpse as a dead Confederate "at a sharpshooter's position." In fact, William Frassantino has convincingly shown that Gardner carried the body to this location from a short distance away and placed the rifle here as a prop.

Comparing this photo to another body in one of Gardner's photos (Photo 7B), Frassantino realized it was the same man by identifying distinctive similarities such as the leg position, the folds in the soldier's clothing and the strap around his neck. The body's original location, the place he was actually killed, was 72 yards WSW of this photo location.

Apparently Gardner found this to be a perfect location for a photo, but it lacked drama. So he decided to haul up the body he had just photographed some 72 yards away, after which he annointed the dead soldier a "sharpshooter," placing the knapsack under his head for a better view of his face.

We know that the body was moved from the site in Photo 7B to this site, instead of the other way around,

because it would have made no sense to move the body from this dramatic location to the more mundane one in Photo 7B.

Gardner's ruse was a tremendous commercial success, and his photo has continued to captivate viewers into this century. In fact, the photo was such a sensation that Gardner spiced up the tale a bit more by spinning a yarn that he returned to the same spot four months later (at the dedication of the National Cemetery) and found the skeleton and the rusted rifle still there and undisturbed.

We know today that the rifle was almost certainly a prop because a similar rifle, and only one, seemed to conspicuously pop up in a number of Gardner's death photos, as if Gardner was packing it around from location to location. (Rifles were valuable. Immediately after the battle, the Union army policed up all weapons on the field even before commencing burial operations). The rifle in any case is not a specialized sniper's rifle, but a standard .58 caliber rifle-musket carried by most Confederate infantrymen.

All that said, there's no doubt that the Confederate was indeed killed in the battle at Devil's Den, and that he was young, with just a hint of a goatee and he was wearing what was called a "shell jacket," a waist-length jacket common to Confederate soldiers. What's odd is that the soldier's body isn't bloated, unlike almost all the other bodies in Gettysburg death scenes - their photos all taken within a day or two of each other.

There's also no doubt that those rocks were piled up by Confederate soldiers, but probably after dark on the night of July 2nd. The wall does indeed face Little Round Top but, at over 600 yards, it would have taken an extremely good shot to hit a bobbing object, such as a Yankee head, at that range.

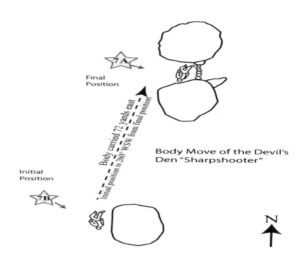

Body Move of the Devil's Den "Sharpshooter"

Photo 7B   *Original location of dead Confederate "Sharpshooter."*

This is where Gardner first came upon the "sharpshooter," who was probably a member of either the 1st Texas or 17th Georgia, lying beside a large boulder on the southern slope of Devils Den. He was probably killed four days earlier, on the afternoon of July 2nd, 1863 in the struggle for Devil's Den. He and his regiment were attacking from right to left in the photo, advancing up the slope toward the Den.

Looking for a more dramatic location for such a valuable body, Gardner and his assistants dragged or carried the corpse 72 yards to the rock wall of Devils Den where the famous "Sniper" photograph (Photo 7A) was taken. The rifle you see in the period photo was probably recovered somewhere in the weeds by Gardner, and packed around throughout the day as a prop for his photos.

The soldier was probably an ordinary infantryman, killed while advancing up the slope toward Devil's Den or the Triangular Field.

Gardner and his assistant, O'Sullivan, took several photos of this soldier at different angles, clearly trying for a sympathetic pose. But then they discovered the rock wall in Devils Den, and so they carried this body 72 yards to where they took the famous 7A photo, promoting the soldier to "a sharpshooter."

Notice that shoe brush near the soldier's body. ... A *shoe* brush?! Lee's army wasn't exactly known for spit and polish.

Question: *Why would he be packing around a shoe brush on a battlefield?*

Pause:

(You have 10 minutes to jot down your answer).

Answer: He probably used it to clean his rifle; making sure dirt, grime and powder didn't jam up the trigger mechanism at an inconvenient time. Most soldiers and hunters keep a shoe brush and/or a tooth brush handy in their gun-cleaning kits today for that same purpose.

Photo 7C   Looking SW toward Devil Den from the Slaughter Pen
Photo taken November 19, 1863 by P. S. Weaver.

This photograph, taken by local photographer Peter Weaver around the time of the dedication of the National Cemetery on November 19, 1863, is the first known photo of Devils Den's massive face. Unfortunately, many of the lower boulders were later blasted to make way for the existing Park road. The early park caretakers were determined to have the road follow the battle lines regardless of any historic damage done in the process.

As discussed previously, on the morning of July 2nd, 1863, troops of the Union III Corps occupied these rocks on the extreme left flank of the Union line which ran north from here across Cemetery Ridge, then Cemetery Hill, and finally Culp's Hill. The troops here were supposed to be deployed on Little Round Top, to the rear of the camera, but their corps commander, Maj.

Gen. Sickles, placed them here, atop the Den, in violation of Meade's orders.

In the late afternoon, waves of Confederate infantry struck Little Round Top and Devils Den. In fierce fighting, the Federals were driven off Devils Den and forced to flee to Little Round Top across a rocky valley called the Slaughter Pen. The Confederates, having seized Devils Den, were unable to take Little Round Top, and so they fell back to cover in and around these rocks, firing in the direction of the camera toward the Union positions on Little Round Top throughout the remainder of the battle.

Devils Den didn't get its name until after the battle.

Photo 7D The massive boulders of Devil's Den

View looking NW. Photo taken Nov. 19th, 1863 by P. S. Weaver.

Here we see one of the classic views of Devil's Den, looking northwest from where the modern Park road runs today. The photo was taken shortly before or after the dedication ceremonies for the National Cemetery on November 19, 1863.

During the battle, Confederate troops drove the Federals off these boulders and then used the Den as a firing position, shooting at Yankees on Little Round Top.

Directly behind the camera is the Slaughter Pen - a rocky valley separating Devils Den from the foot of Big Round Top.

I have no information on who these women are, and why they merited a photograph, but it's a good possibility that they're widows of Union officers killed in the battle.

One woman who might be among them, though she wasn't a widow, is Katherine May Hewitt. She was secretly engaged to Maj. Gen. John Reynolds, the highly respected I Corps commander. Their engagement was secret because he was a Protestant and she a Catholic, and her family would disapprove.

When the war came, she vowed that if he was killed that she would enter a convent. He was indeed killed on the first day's fighting at Gettysburg (see Chapter 2), and she did become a nun, joining the St. Joseph Central House of the Order of Daughters of Charity.

Photo 7E   Little Round Top as seen from Devil's Den
View looking E. Photo taken by Gibson around July 6th or 7th, 1863.

These are two shots of Little Round Top from similar locations. The hazy originals of these photos, taken just three or four days after the battle, shows Gardner was having trouble with the rainy weather. For that reason, I'm showing these skies as being nearly white. Still, the shots give us a good look at what the base of Little Round Top looked like during the battle.

Though you can't see it from these photos, Plum Run Creek runs left to right along this valley. At various times during the hot day of July 2nd, 1863, the creek was a source of desperately needed water for both sides, depending on which side controlled the creek at the time.

The ground depicted in these photos figure prominently in the inner-related struggles for both Little Round Top and Devils Den. During the final stage of the fighting in the Slaughter Pen area, the 2nd Georgia infantry and most likely elements of the 44th and 48th Alabama infantry (by then advancing from right to left), confronted devastating fire here from Union reinforcements - the 40th New York and 6th New Jersey infantry, as well as two guns from Smith's battery, the 4th New York Artillery.

Photo 7F   Little Round Top as seen from Devil's Den
View looking E. Photo taken by Gibson around July 6th or 7th, 1863.

Photo 7G   Dead Confederate at western edge of the Triangular Field

View looking NW toward G. W. Weikert farm. Photo taken by Gibson around July 6th or 7th, 1863.

This site is today hidden in tall grass at the southwestern edge of the Triangular Field, a three acre, rock-lined field directly west of Devil's Den. The photo looks directly west, and the location is about 30 yards southwest of Photo 7B, the original location of the dead soldier in the "Sharpshooter" photo.

George W. Weikert bought this field in 1862. Someone, maybe Weikert himself, constructed a triangular-shaped stone fence around the field prior to the battle. Its interior is far too rocky to be planted, and too small to be used for cattle pasture; so he probably used the field as a hog or sheep pen. To save work, he incorporated the large boulders into his stone fence whenever possible.

(There being numerous mentions in battle reports about a stone fence on the western side of the field, but no mention of the fence on the eastern side, Frassantino speculates that the eastern side may have been fenced with wood, and quickly torn down by Union soldiers for fortifications early on July 2nd.)

The dead Confederate in this photo was probably a Texan. The 1st Texas of Robertson's brigade attacked from a southerly direction (left to right in the photo), and later Benning's Georgia brigade advanced in support, but from the west, heading generally toward the camera.

Once the Confederates seized Houcks Ridge and Devils Den, and throughout July 3rd, Benning's 15th and 17th Georgia regiments occupied this area. No doubt it was the Georgians who gathered the firewood you see in the photo. They likely crawled under those rocks to give them some shade. The fact they left a dead comrade lay next to them for the next day and a half without at least covering him is another indication that the corpse was from a different unit - likely the 1st Texas.

Back in the distance, you can see a wooden structure, which is almost certainly George Weikert's barn.

Photo 7H   Looking SW towards Slyder farm from south end of Devil's Den
Photo taken by C. J. Tyson in 1867.

This photo, taken atop Devil's Den, four years after the battle, looks southwest toward a farm owned in 1863 by John Slyder. The farm still exists today, now called "The Granite Farm."

On the immediate left is the entrance to the Slaughter Pen - a confusing maze of rocks, thorn-covered weeds, and marshy ground, with Plum Run creek running through its center.

In the late afternoon of July 2, 1863, two regiments of Brig. Gen. Evander Law's Alabama brigade - the 15th and 47th Alabama - together with the 4th and 5th Texas infantry of Jerome Robertson's brigade, trotted from the distant tree line across the open ground beyond that near row of tall trees, heading toward Little Round Top. The two Alabama regiments veered right (left in the photo) toward Big Round Top, whereas the Texans attacked directly across the Slaughter Pen.

Soon thereafter, another wave of Confederate infantry - a brigade commanded by Brig. Gen. Henry Benning - advanced in support. One of those regiments was the 2nd Georgia infantry, which advanced northeastward into the Slaughter Pen from the approximate vicinity of the gap in those tall trees, the regiment's right flank covering much of the rocky terrain that dominates this view.

The next day, July 3rd, during Lee's climatic attack on Cemetery Ridge, a Union cavalry brigade guarded the army's left flank in that tree line you see on the left. Twenty-six-year-old Elon Farnsworth, promoted to brigadier general just five days earlier, commanded the brigade. But Farnsworth's jug-eared division commander, Brig. Gen. Judson Kilpatrick (known as "Kill-Patrick" or "Kill Cavalry") was on the scene. Hearing the exciting news of the Confederate repulse on Cemetery Ridge, and probably exaggerated accounts of Brig. Gen. George Custer's dashing attack several miles away at East Cavalry Field, Kilpatrick feared he was missing out on the glory. So he ordered Farnsworth to make a suicidal attack more or less in this direction against Confederate Law's infantry brigade.

When Farnsworth protested the order - cavalry attacking infantry across rocky terrain was suicidal - Kilpatrick called him a coward. Farnsworth made the attack, attacking from left to right in the photo, past the Slyder farm. But seeing he was trapped by waiting Confederate infantry, he and his troopers galloped in this direction, only to be confronted by another firing squad of Confederate infantry. Shot five times, Farnsworth refused to surrender, and bled out probably somewhere just beyond those trees. The attack-fiasco was the last major action of the Battle of Gettysburg.

Brig. Gen. Elon J. Farnsworth

Brig. Gen. Judson Kilpatrick

7A   7B

7C   7D

7E   7F

7G   7H

8   Slaughter Pen

What Happened

The boulder-strewn Slaughter Pen encompasses the valley between Big Round Top and Devil's Den. As the valley runs farther north between Little Round Top and Houck's Ridge, the boulders disappear, the valley's name changes to the Plum Run Valley. Through the center of the valley runs a small creek called Plum Run.

As the 4th and 5th Texas and the 4th Alabama of Brig. Gen. Jerome Robertson's brigade advanced into this rocky, swampy, thorn-covered morass on the late afternoon of July 2nd, 1863, it was impossible to maintain a battleline. They were in the very eye of the storm with thousands of soldiers locked in individual combat to the left on Devil's Den, and also on the right on Little Round Top. Robertson's men were taking incoming canister from the Union artillery on Devil's Den, and their path in the valley was blocked by the 4th Maine regiment to their left front.

In fierce fighting, the Confederates pushed the 4th Maine back up Houck's Ridge. But soon Southerners' path in the Slaughter Pen was again blocked, this time by the big, 600-man regiment of the 40th New York, rushed here from the Wheatfield as reinforcements. The two sides poured volley after volley into each other, until eventually the entire Union line on Houcks Ridge collapsed, and the Federals were forced to retreat to the relative safety of Little Round Top.

Photo 8A Confederate dead at NW base of Big Round Top, next to the Slaughter Pen.
Taken by Gibson & Gardner approximately July 6th, 1863.

Photo 8B *Confederate dead in the Slaughter Pen at base of Big Round Top*
View looking SE. Photo taken by Gardner, probably July 6th or 7th, 1863.

It's hard to see them, but there are at least four dead Confederates in this photo. The view looks across what is today the Devil's Den parking lot, and directly into the Slaughter Pen with the foot of Big Round Top in the background.

Walking around in the middle of the Slaughter Pen is nearly impossible (Believe me!) due to the jumble of sharp boulders of every size, the thickets and thorns, and the spongy soil on either side of Plum Run creek, which runs through the middle of the valley. It's hard to believe that a regiment of infantry fought its way through that morass.

As usual, the dead Confederates here were labeled "sharpshooters" by the photographer, Gardner. In fact, both armies departed this area by the time Gardner arrived, so there was no way Gardner could have known how these soldiers died or what they were doing when they were killed.

Most likely these were ordinary Confederate infantryman, attacking from right to left in the photo on the afternoon of July 2nd, 1863. They were probably from the 4th Texas on its way toward Little Round Top when it tangled with the 4th Maine as well as Federal artillery on top of the Den; or they might have been from later-arriving regiments, the 2nd Georgia and 44th and 48th Alabama, which collided with the 40th New York.

The following day, July 3rd, the Confederates held Devil's Den and Houck's Ridge, and the Federals held Little Round Top. Undoubtedly there was some sniping going on, but both sides had all night to fortify their positions and so it's unlikely that there were many sniper casualties on July 3rd. For among other reasons, it's a long way - 600 yards in some cases - from Devil's Den to the summit of Little Round Top, making it very hard to actually hit anything, at least with iron sights.

Photo 8C   Confederate dead in the Slaughter Pen at base of Big Round Top
View looking SE. Photo taken by Gardner, probably July 6th or 7th, 1863.

This is almost the same scene as the photo on the left (Photo 8B), except this one looks more to the left, and it's a bit closer to the foot of Big Round Top.

The struggle for Devils Den began at approximately 4:30pm and continued for about an hour and a half. Finally threatened with envelopment, Union forces grudgingly relinquished their position, leaving the entire Den to the Confederates.

Though the Slaughter Pen was occupied by Confederate soldiers for roughly 24 hours, the exigencies of battle and the nearby presence of hostile forces did not allow the opportunity to conduct adequate burial operations. Thus when Union burial details first ventured into Devils Den on July 4th, the vast majority of those killed during the second day's fighting, both Union and Confederate, still lay uncovered.

Because the initial efforts of the Northern squads were directed toward the internment of their own dead, the Confederate soldiers in this vicinity lay unburied until July 5th or 6th.

This photo is one of the most famous views recorded at Gettysburg. However, for many years the scene was identified as being at the foot of Little Round Top, not Big Round Top. Only when field investigation uncovered the split rock appearing at the wood line (left-center) was the true location established as being at the foot of Big Round Top.

Photos 8D & 8E Confederate Dead at north edge of pond in the Slaughter Pen
View looking NE. Photo taken by Gardner, probably July 6th or 7th, 1863.

The two dead Confederate soldiers seen here, adjacent to the massive wall of boulders of Devil's Den and lying in the marshy area around Plum Run creek, were probably members of either the 44th or 48th Alabama infantry, killed during the struggle for the Den on July 2, 1863.

The soldiers were attacking toward Little Round Top, the foothill of which you can see in the background. Gardner took this photo four or five days after they had been killed. Their bodies, laying out in the rain and heat, are bloated.

This is a close-up of the same dead soldier who appears in Photo 8D. Note that the rifle, likely a prop carried from location to location by the photographers, has been slightly moved between the two photos. (All weapons were policed up immediately after the battle, well before the Federals got around to burying the dead. Citizens caught gathering rifles could and did find themselves impressed onto burial details).

After lying there for four days, bloating has distorted the man's face. His pockets have been rifled - standard procedure after any battle. The haversack around his neck was his ammo pouch, unlike Union soldiers who generally carried their ammo on their belts. Notice the rifle's been slightly moved from the above photo.

The name "Slaughter Pen" was undoubtedly first heard by Gardner's men from members of Union burial details or from Alford R. Waud (a sketch artist for Harpers weekly) whom they met in the area.

Photo 8F   *Dead Confederate in the Slaughter Pen*
View looking E.   Photo taken by Gardner, probably July 6th or 7th, 1863.

This photo is within a few yards of Photo 8D and 8E's location. The photographer, Gardner, as usual labeled this soldier a "sharpshooter." In fact, this Confederate, his body bloated from having laid out in the rain four or five nights, was probably an infantryman from either the 4th Texas which swept past this area on its way toward Little Round Top, or from three later arriving regiments - the 2nd Georgia and the 44th and 48th Alabama.

Here's a quote which I lifted from one of Frassantino's books, the official battle report by Col. William Perry of the 44th Alabama regiment:

"As the men emerged from the forest into the valley [Slaughter Pen]... they received a deadly volley at short range, which in a few seconds killed or disabled one fourth their number. Halting without an order from me, and availing themselves of the shelter which the rocks supported, they returned fire. Such was their extreme exhaustion, having marched without interruption 24 miles to reach the battlefield, and advanced at a double quick step fully a mile to engage the enemy, that I hesitated for an instant to order them immediately forward. Perceiving very soon, however, that the enemy were giving way, I rushed forward, shouting to them to advance. It was with the greatest difficulty that I could make myself heard or understood above the din of battle. The order was, however, extended along the line, and was promptly obeyed. The men sprang forward over the rocks, swept the position, and took possession of the Heights, capturing 40 or 50 prisoners along with the battery [Smith's 4th New York] among the cliffs."

The 44th Alabama left 24 dead on the field, not including wounded.

Originals

8A

8B

8C

8D

8E

8F

9 Trostle Farm & Emmitsburg Road

What Happened

On the morning of July 2nd, the Army of the Potomac commander, Gen. George Meade, deployed his forces along Cemetery Ridge, facing west. In doing so, as we have by now discussed many times, he assigned III Corps commander, Maj. Gen. Dan Sickles, the position along the southern portion of the ridge, including Little Round Top. But Sickles didn't like his position and so, without bothering to inform Meade, he scooted his line out a little farther; but it still wasn't quite right and so he scooted it out a little more, and then a little more, until finally his corps was clear out on Emmitsburg Road, all alone a half mile out in front of the Union line, with its flanks "in the air" (unprotected).

Worse, at a peach orchard where the Wheatfield Road meets Emmitsburg Road, his position bent into a salient or corner, creating a sharp right angle or an "L" shape in his line. Salients are militarily weak because they allow attackers to fire not only into the enemy line facing them, and also into the backs of defenders facing to the right or left.

Meade, aghast, discovered Sickle's deployment too late - just as the Confederates launched their massive attack. The III Corps was stuck where it was, and although the III Corps troops fought well, often valiantly, eventually the entire corps was broken and driven back in total disarray to Cemetery Ridge.

In the mist of the collapse, one of the Federal artillery batteries at the Peach Orchard, commanded by Capt. John Bigelow, received orders to fall back to the Trostle farm and "hold at all costs" - the standard order of the day for Federal troops.

Bigelow deployed his six guns across Trostle Lane from the Trostle barn and farm house. Sickles,

Capt. John Bigelow

who had been using the area as a headquarters, was by now wounded and out of action.

As the Confederates launched a massive attack across Emmitsburg Road, most of them turned north to wipe out the remaining Federals along the road. But one regiment, the 21st Mississippi, peeled off and advanced down Trostle Lane, intent on seizing Biglow's guns.

Bigelow's men pumped round after round of canister into the advancing Confederates, but they simply closed ranks and kept coming, shooting every horse in sight - without horses the cannon couldn't be withdrawn. About to be overrun, Bigelow ordered a withdrawal. Then he fell wounded. His bugler, Pvt. Charles Reed, raced up to rescue him - an act that earned him the Medal of Honor.

Maj Gen. Daniel E. Sickles

The artillerymen frantically tried pull their guns out, but the guns were blocked by a stone wall to their rear and, with so few horses, the Federals were lucky to escape with just two of their six guns.

The 21st Mississippi then continued up Trostle Lane toward Cemetery Ridge, where it encountered and mauled yet another Yankee battery. But eventually, overwhelming Union reinforcements drove the Mississippians all the way back to Emmitsburg Road, forcing them to abandon Bigelow's cannon in the process.

Photo 9A   *Trostle Barn and dead artillery horses of the 9th Massachusetts*
View looking NW. Photo taken by O'Sullivan, probably July 6th or 7th, 1863.

Both of these photos were taken just three days after the battle.

The dead horses in this photo belonged to Bigelow's 9th Massachusetts Artillery Battery. They were shot by surging Confederates to prevent the Federals from withdrawing their cannon. By the time the photo was taken, the dead men had been buried; only the horse carcasses remained.

The Trostle barn area served as the headquarters of the III Corps commander, Sickles - the man responsible for the Union debacle at Emmitsburg Road, the Peach Orchard, and Devils Den. Near the far corner of this barn, out in an open field, Sickles was desperately trying to rally his men when a cannon ball fragment neatly clipped his leg, leaving his horse untouched. Lifted from his horse and placed on a gurney, Sickles defiantly lit up a cigar as he was carried away.

His leg was amputated 30 minutes later, and for some reason he had the leg put on display in the Washington DC National Museum of Health and Medicine. A sentimental man, Sickles had grown attached to his leg, and on occasion, usually slightly inebriated and in the arms of one or two young ladies, the old general would pay his leg a visit at the museum. It might still be there, in case you'd like to swing by and visit it the next time you're in Washington. Tell them I sent you.

Note the Confederate cannon hole in the barn's brick, just below the diamond.

Photo 9B (Opposite page)
This photo of the house was taken almost from the same location as the previous one, but in a different direction. From the Peach Orchard, the 424 men of the 21st Mississippi cut across the fields, heading toward Trostle Lane. Blocking their path was Bigelow's six-gun battery, deployed in a semi-circle on the lane next to the Trostle house and barn. Bigelow's orders were to hold at all costs.

The Mississippians charged, intent on seizing the guns. Bigelow, who was wounded in the fray, later recalled how his canister mowed the enemy down but, "yelling like demons," the Confederates threw themselves at the battery, and eventually drove off Bigelow's cannoneers and captured four guns. But the cannoneers' stubborn fight bought desperately needed time for Union forces on Cemetery Ridge to slap together a new defensive line.

In the process of attacking the battery, the Mississippians shot and bayonetted the artillery horses - 50 in all - standard infantry procedure when attacking artillery to prevent the horses from pulling away the cannons. The Mississippians lost 34% of their men in the Gettysburg battle, many of them here.

Photo 9B Dead artillery horses in front of Trostle house.
View looking NE. Photo taken by O'Sullivan, probably July 6th or 7th, 1863.

Sketch drawn by Capt. John Biglow of the fight at the Trostle Farm. (The commentary is upside down from the drawing).

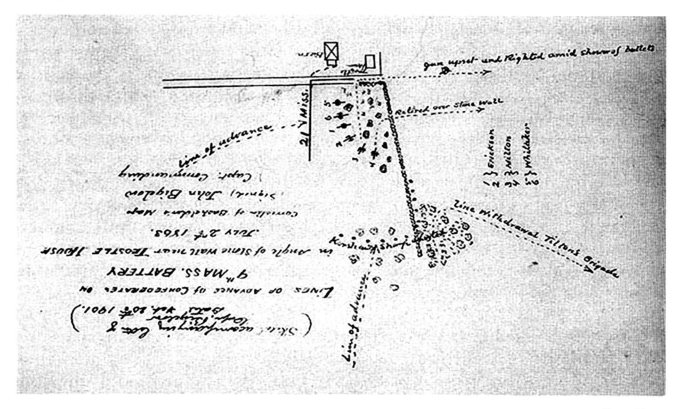

Photo 9C   Emmitsburg Road - looking NE from the Klingle house

View looking NE toward town. Photo taken by Mumper in 1889. Photo owned by William Frassantino.

Here, a quarter century after the battle, we're looking northeast up Emmitsburg Road toward Gettysburg.

Just off camera to the right of the photo is the Daniel Klingle house and farm. Klingle was witness to the Union I Corps' advance up Emmitsburg Road on July 1st, and watched as they tore down his fence to the west of the road (camera left) and advanced at the double-quick across the Spangler and McMillan farm fields on their way to the first day's battlefield northwest of town. In the evening "14 to 16" wounded Confederates were brought to Klingle's house, where the family cared for them through the night.

After repeated warnings from Union officers, on the 2nd day the Klingel family - his wife and two children - left the farm, heading by way of the Trostle farm to the foot of Little Round Top. Klingle was taken up to the Union signal station on Little Round Top, where he helped identify roads and terrain features. When the hill came under fire from a Confederate gun on Warfield Ridge he slipped away and returned to his family. They made their way to a friend's house near Rock Creek, where they waited out the battle.

When he returned after the battle he found his farm devastated and littered with dead bodies that lay all around the house. Two were just inside the gate, and two others under the porch where they must have crawled for shelter before dying of their wounds. One shattered tree in Klingel's orchard concealed four dead

soldiers huddled around a cooking pan with food still in it.

In the right mid-distance of the photo you can see the Codori Farm which was about in the center of two of Maj. Gen. George Pickett's Confederate brigades as their lines swept past the farm from camera-left to camera-right on the climatic 3rd day of the battle. Picket's third brigade, commanded by Brig. Gen. James Kemper, crossed the road with probably its right flank about here, just in front of the camera position.

The house and barn you see in the photo on the left were not there at the time of the battle and are not there now. Instead there was another house, a one-story log cabin owned by a Peter Rogers, just on this side of that tall monument on the left - the 1st Massachusetts monument. Incredibly, Rogers and his granddaughter, Josephine Miller, remained in the house during the battle, baking bread for the men and caring for many wounded in the cellar.

After the war the 1st Massachusetts infantry regiment, which held this section of the road on the 2nd day's fighting, dedicated its monument on the Rogers farm. The men invited Josephine and paid for her trip back to Gettysburg for the dedication, where she was presented with a gold badge as a "tribute of their gratitude for her kindly services." In the right far-distance of the photo you can see the northern edge of Cemetery Ridge and Ziegler's Grove, which anchored the right flank of the Union line on July 2nd and 3rd.

Photo 9D   Emmitsburg Road - looking SW from the Klingle house

View looking SW towards the Peach Orchard Photo taken by Mumper in 1889. Photo owned by William Frassantino.

This shot is a companion to the previous photo, but looking in the opposite direction, away from Gettysburg. Here we're looking southwest down Emmitsburg Road toward the Sherfy farm and the Peach Orchard.

The Klingle house, just out of view to the left of the camera, served as the right flank of the III Corp's battle-line on July 2nd. The Federals manned the east (camera left) side of the road, facing the on-rushing Confederates. The Confederates charged across this road, driving the Federal line back behind the house, and finally smashing the Union line in heavy fighting.

The trees of the Sherfy Peach Orchard are visible in the far background on the left side of the road, as are the

Sherfy farm buildings on the immediate right of road. The Sherfy orchard, known as The Peach Orchard, was a site of heavy fighting on July 2nd, as was the entire area around the Sherfy buildings, and all the way up the road to this photo location.

On July 3rd, during the climatic Confederate assault on Cemetery Ridge, the brigade of Col. David Lang's Florida brigade, along with Brig. Gen. Cadmus Wilcox's Alabama brigade, crossed this road again, this time on their way to attack the southern end of Cemetery Ridge on July 3rd. But by the time they joined the battle, the main assault was already collapsing and Lang and Wilcox were soon forced to retreat.

Lang's Florida brigade included a preacher's son, Pvt. Lewis Paine,(aka Lewis Powell) who would be wounded in the hand and captured in this attack. He was brought to Pennsylvania College in Gettysburg where his wound was dressed. He soon escaped, helped by a friendly nurse, whereupon he joined Mosby's Raiders, a Confederate semi-guerrilla group. Somehow he ended up in Washington DC, where he joined the conspiracy to kill Abraham Lincoln.

His short be eventful life ended when he was hanged for the Lincoln assassination almost exactly two years to the day after his capture here in the Gettysburg battle.

Lewis Powell

Modern View of Klingle House

Photo 9E   Emmitsburg Road
View looking SW toward the Codori Farm.
Photo taken by Tipton & Co. 1876-1877

This photo, taken 13 or 14 years after the battle, also looks southward down Emmitsburg Road as does Photo 9D. But this time the camera position is much farther north, very close to Gettysburg, behind the camera. The Copse of Trees, the unofficial target of the Confederate's attack against Cemetery Ridge on the 3rd day, is about 200 yards off camera to the left.

This view along that road looks southwestward toward the Nicolas Codori house on the left. Codori's slaughterhouse sits on the right side of the road in the open fields. It was over this stretch of post-and rail fencing along Emmitsburg Road that the Confederate brigades of Richard B. Garnett and Lewis A. Armistead, Pickett's division, crossed from right to left in the climatic attack on the third day at Gettysburg. The attacking lines divided to pass the Codori house and then re-connected again on the other side, stopping to redress their lines in the midst of blistering artillery fire, prior to making the final assault on Cemetery Ridge. Both brigade com-

manders and hundreds of their men were killed in the final assault.

These fences had a great deal to do with breaking the Confederate attack in this area. All along this fence row, including where the camera is located, the Confederates had to either climb over the fences on both sides of the road, or take time as a group to push them down while Federal bullets where whacking the fence "like hail." It was just too tempting to take cover, so many or most of the attackers in this section simply remained at the road and continued firing, while only the bravest of the brave rose up, continued over both fences, and charged up the slope into the hell on Cemetery Ridge. Most who went over those fences had to know they weren't coming back.

Farther south along the road, past the Codori farm, the fences were not a problem on the third day's final assault because they had been torn down in the previous day's fighting.

Photo 9F   The Peach Orchard

View looking SE at intersection of Emmitsburg Road and Wheatfield Road. Photo taken by Mumper in 1889. Photo owned by William Frassantino.

In 1889 a monument was constructed for the 63rd Pennsylvania regiment on the opposite side of Emmitsburg Road from the Peach Orchard. This photo was taken from the rigging of that monument. It's the first known photograph of the Peach Orchard, an area of intense fighting on the second day of the battle. The view looks toward the northwestern corner of the orchard, with Wheatfield Road running east away from the camera. Directly in front of the camera, but not in view, is Emmitsburg Road.

When Maj. Gen. Dan Sickles, advanced his entire III Corps off Cemetery Ridge almost a half mile to this position, the Peach Orchard, it was the farthest point of his line. He packed the left side of Wheatfield Road with cannon facing the orchard. And from the edge of this orchard his line made a sharp angle north (camera-left), with his troops manning several hundred yards of Emmitsburg Road up to the Klingle house. Unfortunately for Sickles and his men, the sharp turn created a "sa-

lient", or "L" shaped bend in their line, making it tactically weak; worse, their flanks were "in the air," meaning unguarded, because the rest of the Union army was still back up on Cemetery Ridge.

Lt. Gen. Longstreet, Lee's best corps commander, hurled waves of Confederate infantry against this vulnerable salient, attacking from behind the camera, and from camera-right through the orchard, breaking Sickles' line and wrecking his corps, which fled in disarray back to Cemetery Ridge.

The orchard belonged to the Sherfy farm, located on the west side of Emmitsburg Road - just off camera to the left . The orchard extended across Wheatfield Road to the left for at least 100 yards.

Originals

9A

9B

9C

9D

9E

9F

10   Rose Farm

What Happened

The fighting south of the John Rose farm on July 2nd, 1863 was likely just one of numerous deadly but unknown "mini-battles" at Gettysburg. It would have remained unknown except for two events: first, this location happened to be one of the first places photographers reached shortly after the battle where bodies still lay unburied; second, over a century later, William Frassantino, a student of Gettysburg photography, figured out exactly where the photographs were taken.

Frassantino's find here, the location of 10 death scene photos taken days after the battle, is arguably his greatest contribution to the history of Gettysburg. Prior to his identifying this location, it was believed that these photos were taken somewhere on the northern part of the battlefield.

Except for three photos at the end of this chapter, all of the dead in these photos are Confederates. Most likely they were Georgians, members of Brig. Gen. Paul Semmes' 1,334 man brigade, which took part in Lee's massive July 2nd wave assault. More specifically, at least according to Frassantino, they were probably of the 53rd or 51st Georgia regiments, although he speculates they might also have been part of the 15th South Carolina, which passed through this area before Semmes' men did. But the 53rd Georgia seems to be the most likely choice.

At around 6:30pm, they attacked eastward across Rose's open pasture, to be met at the tree line of Rose Woods by the 2nd Delaware Regiment of Col. John Brooke's brigade.

Judging from the 44 of bodies here, the fighting was substantial (A rule of thumb is to expect two or three wounded for every man killed, so there may have been over a hundred Confederate casualties here). The Confederates drove the Federals eastward back to and through Wheatfield, which itself became an inferno.

In all, Semmes' brigade lost 432 dead, wounded and missing that day (a 32% casualty rate), including Semmes, who was mortally wounded in the Wheatfield. Carried to the rear, he murmured to a war correspondent as he lay dying that he considered it an honor to die for his country.

Brig. Gen. Paul J. Semmes

Photo 10A   *Confederate dead at SW edge of Rose Woods*
View looking SE. Photo taken by Gardner, probably July 5th or 6th, 1863.

Frassantino wandered the Gettysburg battlefield for five years, looking for the "split rock" in this photo, before discovering it here, south of the Rose Farm and nowhere near the northern part of the battlefield where it was assumed to be. His discovery of this one particular rock was no small feat when you consider that Gettysburg grows rocks like Saudi Arabia grows oil.

As in the other photos, we're looking at Confederate dead of Semmes' Brigade, killed by Federals of Brooke's brigade as the Rebels advanced from across the open field toward that tree line.

Body Layout

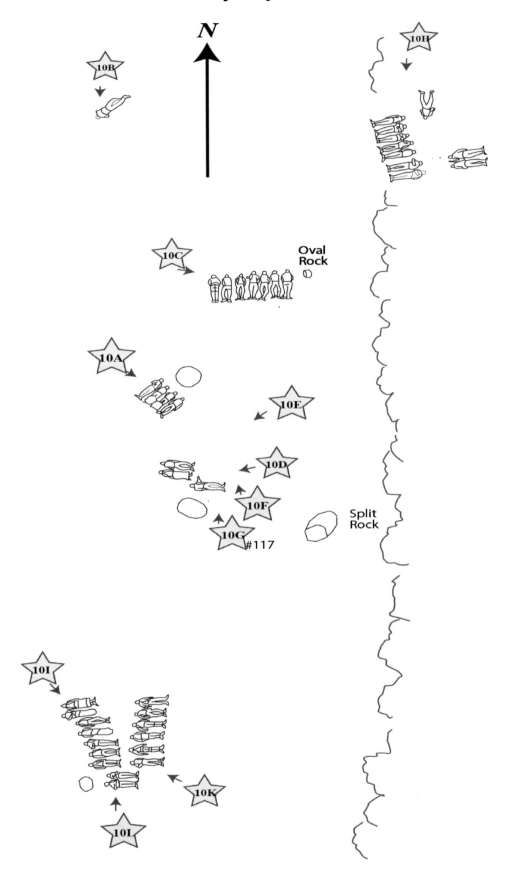

Photo 10B Dead Confederate at SW edge of Rose Woods

View looking S. Photo taken by O'Sullivan, probably July 5th or 6th, 1863.

Originally titled "War, effect of a shell on a Confederate soldier," The soldier's arm has been ripped from its socket and a left hand - presumably his - lies next to him, along with a canteen with a bullet hole in it, plus a rifle and an artillery shell. All three were probably props, picked up elsewhere on the field, which Gardner used to increase the photo's drama.

Frassantino speculates that the gaping wound in the man's stomach may have been the work of scavenging hogs rather than artillery fire. It's possible. Wild hogs feeding on the dead and wounded soldiers were indeed a curse on most Civil War battlefields, although it's odd that the hog or hogs devoted all their attention to just this one body, as none of the other bodies in any of the

photos here or elsewhere seem to have been similarly disfigured.

Like the other bodies photographed at the southwestern edge of the Rose Wood's, this soldier was probably a member of either the 51st or 53rd Georgia regiment of Semmes' brigade, killed in the July 2nd assault against that wood line. Now lying dead and dismembered on this field, his family back in Georgia would be worrying by the time this photo was taken; no doubt they had just heard the news about a great battle fought at a place called Gettysburg.

Photo 10C   Confederate dead at SW edge of Rose Woods
View looking SE. Photo taken by Gibson, probably July 5th or 6th, 1863.

Though Frassantino used the split-rock in Photo 10A to find this entire photo location, my Eureka moment came when I saw that strange rock in the photo near the head of the last Confederate in the row. The rock is called "the Oval Rock." It's still there today.

In the photo you can barely see a fence line in the wooded background. Frassantino speculates that, because fencing usually borders rather than enters woods, it's likely the Confederates pulled up the fencing and used it as a barricade inside the treeline on the morning of July 3rd.

It's also likely that all seven dead Confederates seen here were killed in a firefight with Brooke's Union brigade, whose troops briefly held a ledge just inside the wood line during the late afternoon of the second day's fighting, before being driven back to the Wheatfield. In the following day and a half, the exhausted Southerners had enough time to line up their comrades for burial, but not enough time to bury them.

While being dragged to this location by his arms, the boy on the end had his pants pulled down, left to be seen that way in a photograph for centuries thereafter.

The Oval Rock today

Photo 10D   Confederate dead at SW edge of Rose Woods
View looking SW. Photo taken by O'Sullivan, probably July 5th or 6th, 1863.

Photo 10D was taken just before Photo 10E, which shows the same bodies, but one now covered in its grave.

Here we're looking southwest toward the southern extension of Seminary Ridge (aka Warfield Ridge), the location from which Semme's brigade launched its attack toward this location here at Rose Woods. The Rose Woods treeline is about 30 yards behind the camera. Semmes' four Georgia regiments, 1,334 men in total, would have advanced toward the camera across those open fields, in line of battle with flags waving. Before the day was out, 432 of them would be killed, wounded or missing, including Semmes, who was mortally wounded.

Note the obviously muddy condition of the earth at the edge of the open grave in the right foreground. It appears the burial crew was busy here in the mist of these camera shots. Note the soldier lying against the rock, and his absence on the second shot (Photo 10E). In all likelihood the body was placed in the grave beside the soldier with the raised knee in Photo 10E in the moments between the two camera shots.

The unpleasant task of burying bodies after battles was often done on an assembly-line basis:

(a) Gather the bodies and lay them out in a row

(b) dig one grave at the end of the line

(c) lay that body in the open hole,

(d) dig an adjoining grave,

(e) cover the first with the dirt from the new hole, and lay the second body in the new hole

(e) Etc, down the row of bodies.

Photo 10E

Photo 10F *Confederate dead at SW edge of Rose Woods*
View looking NW. Photo taken by Gardner, probably July 5th or 6th, 1863.

This is the same line of dead shown in Photo 10G. Also, in the far right background of this shot you can see the beginning of the line of bodies photographed in Photo 10C. (Gardner seems to have gone out of his way to include the naked buttocks of that last body in the line).

The open grave in the left foreground is probably meant for the soldier with his knee up.

In both this photo and Photo 10G, the Sherfy Peach Orchard can just barely be seen on the horizon beyond. But clearly the orchard was only included by accident. Strangely, and unfortunately, it would be decades before any photographer took a photo of either the Peach Orchard or Cemetery Ridge, both areas are of great historical interest today.

That wagon in the photo served as Gardner's darkroom. Each time he took a photo he had to climb inside the wagon to develop his negative, which took about 10 minutes.

The blankets you see lying around were probably blanket-rolls, carried everywhere by Confederates, including into battle. After their death, the burial details used the blankets to drag the bodies to this central location for burial.

10G

This is the same view as Photo 10F, but a wide angle shot.

Photo 10H Confederate dead at SW edge of Rose Woods
View looking S. Photo taken by O'Sullivan, probably July 5th or 6th, 1863. Photo owned by William Frassantino.

Unlike the other death scenes on the Rose Farm, these soldiers are lying farther inside the woods, rather than out in the open field. Note that there's a grave with a marker just visible at the tree line at the left of the photo.

Like the ones you see in the rest of these photos, these bodies were no doubt gathered for burial by their Confederate comrades on the morning of July 3rd, but they didn't have time to finish the job.

The photo is hazy, probably because it was taken in the shade of the trees. Note the canteen with the bullet hole - the same one in Photo 10B.

Photo 10I Unfinished Confederate Graves
Photo taken by Gardner, probably July 5th or 6th, 1863. Location unknown except probably on the Rose Farm lane.

Although the exact location of these photo is unknown, it was very likely taken on the lane leading from Emmitsburg Road to the Rose Farm. Note the tidy, whitewashed fence in the background. It probably ran down the Rose lane.

These unfinished graves were no doubt dug by their comrades who didn't have time to complete the task. These men were from Brig. Gen. Joseph Kershaw's South Carolina brigade.

Photo 10J Confederate dead at SW edge of Rose Woods
View looking SSE. Photo taken by O'Sullivan, probably July 5th or 6th, 1863.

Of the series of death photos here on the Rose Farm, this photo is probably the sharpest.

On July 2nd, Brooke's Federals had fought their way through the woods to the fence you see here, facing this open pasture on Rose's farm. Semmes counterattacked across the field, where these men were killed, eventually driving Brooke back through the Wheatfield.

More photos were taken of the dead in this southern end of the Rose Farm than any other location on the Gettysburg battlefield. But, ironically, the fighting here is barely noted in Gettysburg histories, and it is only because of these photos that we know something happened here.

Not only was Semmes mortally wounded in fighting later at the Wheatfield, but Brooke was also severely wounded. Consequently neither man filed battle reports. As Frassantino pointed out, even if they had filed reports, probably neither possessed the literary skills of college-professor Col. Joshua Chamberlain of the 20th Maine, who went on to create a legend around his regiment's fight - a relatively minor affair in the bigger scheme of events at Gettysburg - whereas the fighting here, probably just as fierce as anything experienced by the 20th Maine, would have remained totally unknown if it were not for these photos.

It's likely that there were other "mini-battles" fought at Gettysburg that we will never know about, such as the unknown location of the photos of the Federal dead at the end of this chapter.

These troops had been on a hard march for almost a month to get here from Virginia, sleeping on the ground at night rolled up in a blanket. Yet their hair is cut short and their beards, the few who have them, are fairly well trimmed. That shows discipline. Despite their motley collection of uniforms, these were not just a bunch of yahoos with guns.

Note that hole in the pants of the body nearest the camera. Because he was bloated, someone apparently cut open his pants to get whatever was in his pocket.

Photo 10K Confederate dead at SW edge of Rose Woods
View looking NW. Photo taken by O'Sullivan, probably July 5th or 6th, 1863.

These bodies, arranged in a "V" formation, are also the subject of Photos 10J and 10L.

Here the camera is facing northwest toward the John Rose house and barn. You can see his peach orchard on the horizon. The Rose Woods is just out of sight to the right of the camera.

As discussed, these soldiers were probably members of either Brig. Gen. Joseph Kershaw's 15th South Carolina brigade or, more likely, the later-arriving 53rd Georgia on the right flank of Semme's brigade. They were attacking from left to right in the photo, and probably clashed with the 2nd Delaware, on the left flank of Brooke's Union brigade, deployed in Rose Woods to the right of the photo.

Note that many of these bodies have their legs tied together, and in some cases their arms. Presumably the ropes made it easier to drag the bodies, or possibly the ropes were used to secure the limbs to keep them from extending outward in rigor mortis, making burial more difficult.

Photo 10L

Another view of the "V" formation, this time looking at the tip of the V.

#1 *Union dead at Gettysburg*
Photo taken by Gardner, probably July 5th or 6th, 1863. Location unknown.

I've included these three photos of Union dead in the Rose Farm chapter, though in fact no one knows where Gardner took these photos, except that he probably took them on the south portion of the battlefield, on either July 5th or 6th, 1863. These are the only known Gettysburg photos of Union dead.

Photos #1 and #2 show the same scene, except one is a close-up and the other a wide-angle.

There are at least 15-16 bodies here, so if we use a rule of thumb of 2-3 times that number wounded, there must have been at least 50 or more Union casualties here. This wasn't just a skirmish.

William Frassantino searched for years but never found this photo location. There are no permanent landmarks to orient on, such as boulders, distant mountains, or buildings. In fact, about the only real clue is that rising hill in the background.

I decided that's a road on the background of Photo #2, though it might have been a fence. Either way it   **#2**

it could be long gone by now. The only thing Frassantino concluded is that, wherever the photos were taken, it was not on the northern side of the battle field as was originally thought. And if Frassantino couldn't find this location after years of searching, it probably can't be found.

Assuming the northern part of the battlefield is

eliminated, and assuming Gardner didn't have time to reach the center of Gettysburg before the Union bodies were buried, then the site of these photos would almost have to be somewhere along Emmitsburg Road, possibly well south of Rose farm along the road where there was minor fighting on July 2nd and 3rd, and where Gardner and his crew would have first encountered the battlefield. The problem with that theory is that there are no reports of Union infantry fighting well south of the Rose Farm - only some fighting by dismounted Union cavalry. But in addition to there being no dead horses around, it's unlikely that cavalrymen with their lighter weapons would have fought out in an open field, bunched up like this. So these are probably infantry.

It appears likely that these were the first photos Gardner's photographic team recorded when they reached Gettysburg. This would easily have taken   at least an hour to produce the five negatives. (I've only included the three best). But were there not also Confederates killed in the fight? Gardner took no pictures of them.

The soldiers' shoes have been removed, usually a strong indication that Confederates occupied this location. But why not take their socks? I would. And where's the Confederates' disgarded shoes? No hats either. I suspect those clothing articles were scooped up by the Federal quartermaster for recycling - meaning that the field was not necessarily occupied by Confederates.

Anyway, the photo's location is a puzzle.

That's a young 2nd Lieutenant in the first and second photos; the one with the shoulder insignia. Even in death his face is handsome enough to be on a coin.

Union Dead

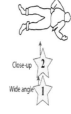

Close-up 2

Wide angle 1

#3

10A 10B Originals 10C

10D 10E 10F

10G 10H 10I

10J 10K 10L

#1 #2 #3

11 Culps Hill

What Happened

It's ironic that many tourists ignore Culps Hill today. Even the Park only includes the hill on its tour guide as an optional (and therefore probably not very important) visit.

But shortly after the battle and for decades thereafter, Culps Hill was one of the most popular tourist attractions here at Gettysburg, primarily because of its bullet-riddled trees, and also because the original Union barricades remained in place here for a long time. But the bullet-riddled trees are gone now, as are the original barricades, and so Culps Hill has become a rather lonely place - just a quiet woods with a bunch of statues.

But it wasn't always that way.

It's also ironic that Culps Hill was actually more important to the Union victory than its much more famous and picturesque cousin to the south, Little Round Top. Culps Hill controlled access to Baltimore Pike, the Federals' supply artery. Little Round Top controlled nothing. If the Confederates had seized Little Round Top, they would have won themselves a dandy view of the western sunset, but not much else. But if they had seized Culps Hill, cutting off the Federal supply line, Meade would have been forced to abandon his prime real estate on Cemetery Ridge, and withdraw to fight Lee elsewhere, possibly with a much different outcome.

On the morning of July 2nd, 10,000 men of the Union XII Corps occupied this hill, facing east. The corps commander, Maj. Gen. Henry Slocum, left it up to his individual brigade commanders to decide whether they wanted to fortify their positions. (At that time of the war, many commanders discouraged fortifications because they feared defensive works made the men timid).

The brigade at the top of Culps Hill was commanded by Brig. Gen. George

Greene's monument on the summit of Culps Hill

Brig. Gen. George S. Greene

Greene, the oldest Union brigadier on the battle, known as "Pap" or "Pappy" to his young troops. An engineer, Pappy definitely believed in fortifications and he knew how to build them. He ordered his troops to make full use of the abundant timber and boulders in the area to construct a wall thick enough to stop a locomotive.

By noon, the solidly fortified and heavily manned Union position on Culps Hill was nearly impregnable. But around 4pm, just before dusk, nervous Union commanders rushed most of the XII Corps troops south to reinforce the battles raging at Little Round Top, the Wheatfield, etc. But the generals overdid it, leaving only Greene's one, lonely, 1,400 man-brigade to defend the entire hill.

Just about then, Confederates attacked Culps Hill. By the thinnest of margins, mainly due to his barricade, Greene managed to hold off assault after assault until nightfall, when the other XII Corps units returned.

The next day, July 3rd, the Confederates again attacked the barricade, turning Culps Hill into one massive, smoke-covered firefight. But they never could take the hill.

Photo 11A   Boulder used by Confederates in front of Greene's line

View looking SW. Photo taken by Brady & Co. around July 15, 1863.

This boulder served as cover and a firing position for the Virginians of Brig. Gen. John Jones' brigade, in their fierce but futile 2-day assault against the solid barricade constructed by the 60th New York regiment, about 70 feet back up the hill (camera-left). In other words, the two sides were slamming away at each other from just 20 yards away.

Seen in the foreground of this picture is the boulder that appears in an oil painting by Edwin Forbes (next page). As is clear from Forbes' painting, this boulder, together with smaller surrounding rocks, served as a shelter for Confederate marksman during the fighting.

In the photo, the photographer assistant is looking east in the direction of Rock Creek, the direction from which the Confederates advanced.

Look how high many of those bullet holes are on the trees! Either shooters weren't aiming or there was so much smoke they couldn't see their targets. Those are Yankee bullet holes, but there are other photos of the trees that indicate the Confederate marksmanship was just as bad.

Almost every teacher and professor discussing the Civil War knowingly states that the reason for the high casualty rate in the Civil War was due to the commanders bunching up their soldiers close ranks, and marching them too close to the enemy, not understanding the greater distance and firepower of the Civil War rifle-musket.

There's no doubting the firepower of a Civil War rifle-musket. Looking at the size of those bullet holes in the trees, you can imagine what they would do if they hit human flesh and bone.

On the other hand, you can see from the grouping of shots here - if you can call it "grouping" - that even from 20 yards away, the combatants' marksmanship was so bad that they were more likely to hit an eagle than the enemy. True, there was a lot of smoke in this battle, but there was a lot of smoke in every Civil War battle. The moral is that Civil War commanders had perfectly good reason to march their troops close to the enemy, because they couldn't hit the broad side of a barn otherwise! And the reason they kept their men in ranks is because that's the only way they could control the formations, which had to be led by voice or drum commands over the roar of battle. Plus, due to the slow reloading capabilities of the weapons (at best, 3 shots a minute), the only way dominate a firefight was to keep the men together, and have them fire on command in an mechanical fashion, one line standing and one line kneeling.

Painting by Edwin Forbes showing the boulder in Photo 11A.

That large rock at the bottom of this painting is the same one in Photo 11A. The Yankees had their own large rock, incorporated into Greene's barricade, as seen at the top of the hill, The woods in the painting appear to be much thinner than they are today at that location. Probably the artist made them thinner to show more of the action.

Photo 11B   Brady assistants sitting in front of 102nd New York's breastworks

View looking SE. Photo taken by the Brady & Co., around July 15th, 1863.

Here we're looking southeastward along the portion of Greene's line occupied on July 2, 1863 by the 78th and 102nd New York Infantry. During the fighting on the evening of July 2, the breastworks at this point were occupied by the left flank of the 102nd New York regiment. Brady's two assistants are gazing eastward over the breastworks in the direction of the Confederate attack.

Photo 11C   In Front of Union Breastworks along Greene's Line
View looking E. Photo taken by Brady & Co., probably around July 15, 1863.

This location is about 50 yards in front of the location of Photo 11B.

Again, notice the bullet holes. All the holes you see here were made by Federals of either the 102nd New York or 78th New York. The Southerners would have been attacking toward the camera, and there's probably an equal number of Confederate bullet holes on the opposite side of the trees. The fellow lying on the ground and playing dead is a Brady assistant. Using his height as a rough guide, some of those bullet holes in the trees must be 30 feet high in the photo, and there might have been more above the photo!

A reporter, Thomas W. Knox, sent a dispatch to the New York Herald on July 9, dated: Gettysburg, July 6, 1863:

"... I find tree after tree scarred from base to limb so thickly that it would have been impossible to place one's hand upon their trunks without covering the marks of a bullet ... Every tree and brush for the distance of half a mile along these woods was nearly as badly marked. The storm of bullets must have been as thick as hailstones in an ordinary storm. How a man could exist in it and come out unhurt is difficult to imagine."

Another visitor in the summer of 1863 wrote a similar description:

"... the trees ... were so pierced that from the roots on the ground for 30 to 40 feet high there was scarcely a space the breath of the hand that escaped the bullet. And a single tree, not more than 1 foot in diameter, over 70 bullet holes were counted; over 30 of these within 6 feet of the ground. ... It seems incredible how any person escape being killed or wounded..."

It was due to these battered trees that Culps Hill was so interesting to early Gettysburg tourists. But today all the pockmarked trees are gone, as are most of the tourists.

Photo 11D   Spanglers Meadow

View looking NE. Photo taken by the Tyson Bros.. 1866. Photo owned by Gettysburg National Park

Fighting on Culps Hill, which began late in the afternoon of July 2nd, picked up again at daybreak on July 3rd, with the Confederates futilely charging against the Federal barricade along the middle and top of the hill, creating a massive gunfight and blanketing the woods in smoke, but making absolutely no progress.

But this photo was taken at the bottom of the hill, and it involved another futile charge, this time by the Federals - the only Federal infantry attack of the three-day battle. It occurred late in the morning of July 3rd, a couple of hours before Lee's massive attack on Cemetery Ridge.

After having been hurriedly dispatched in late afternoon on July 2nd to assist in the fighting around Little Round Top, Union Col. Silas Colgrove's brigade returned here to Culps Hill after dark, where the Federals now found themselves facing a strong Confederate line (four battered but still dangerous regiments) at the wood line at the far end of this photo.

By daylight on July 3rd, it was clear to everyone on location that an attack across this open meadow would be suicidal. But down came an order, delivered by a messenger from the XII Corps commander, Maj. Gen. Henry Slocum, to make the attack *if* it was feasible. Unfortunately, the vital word "if" got lost in the translation. The way Colgrove heard it, the order was to make the attack, period. He sent a message to Mudge to make the attack.

At approximately 10am on July 3, the 2nd Massachusetts infantry, led by Lt. Col. Charles Mudge, accompanied by the 27th Indiana on his right - some 650 men in total - got the order. Mudge asked the messenger if he was sure that was the order. The messenger said he was.

Mudge muttered, "Well, it's murder, but it's the order." Then he called his men into formation and commenced the doomed attack across the open swale.

This photo, taken three years after the battle, looks northeast across Spangler's Meadow from the direction of Baltimore Pike. It was from the woods on the extreme right and along a line running parallel to the fence traversing the center of the scene, that Mudge and the two regiments began their doomed assault.

The Confederate unleashed a storm of fire. Halfway into Spangler's Meadow the 2nd Massachusetts made the fatal mistake of stopping to fire back, and was shredded by incoming fire. But the 2nd Massachusetts pressed forward with Mudge in the lead. Soon Mudge was killed with a shot to the neck. The 27th Indiana then advanced, drawing the Confederates' fire and allowing the decimated 2nd Mass troops to flee to the woods to the camera-left, leaving 136 bodies writhing on the field - a 43% casualty rate. The 27th Indiana, having lost over 100 men in a few moments, also turned back.

Col. Charles Mudge

Incredibly, the Confederates, hoping to take advantage of the Yankees' confusion, launched their own attack across the field, which did nothing but add another 100 bodies on the field.

That pretty much ended the fighting here on Culps Hill. The battle now shifted back to Cemetery Ridge where Lee would soon make his climatic attack.

Originals

11A

11B

11C

11D

12   East Cemetery Hill

What Happened

On July 1st, 1863, Maj. Gen. Oliver Howard observed from the roof of the Fahnestock building in Gettysburg as his troops fought west and north of Gettysburg. With the death of Maj. Gen. John Reynolds early in the battle, the one-armed Howard assumed the role of Union commander until Gen. George Meade arrived. Howard, like Buford before him, realized that the "good ground" was southeast of Gettysburg, on Cemetery Hill and Cemetery Ridge, and so even though his forces on the outskirts of town were slowing being crushed, and even though they sent urgent messages requesting support, Howard refused to commit all his reserves to the battle. Instead he retained about a third of his available force on Cemetery Hill, preparing it as a last redoubt until Meade and the rest of the Union army could reach the town.

His decision to hold Cemetery Hill at all costs was one of the pivotal and relatively unsung events that won the battle for the Union. When the demoralized Union forces north and west of town broke and fled through town, they instinctively headed for Cemetery Hill; and there they found order, determination, and plenty of artillery support. When the rest of the Union army reached the scene, Cemetery Hill became a fortress, packed hub to hub with cannon.

Late the next day, at around dusk on July 2nd, East Cemetery Hill became the target of the final lash in Lee's wave attack that began far on the south end of the Union line at Little Round Top. Here soldiers from North Carolina and Louisiana attacked from town, advancing across open ground toward East Cemetery Hill under blistering cannon fire.

The Southerners managed to break through the Union infantry guarding the bottom of the hill and, incredibly, some of them even reached the hill's summit near the cemetery gate where, in savage hand-to-hand fighting in the twilight, the Confederates seized some of the Union cannon guarding the hillside. The exhausted attackers had done all they could do. Now they waited for reinforcements to carry on the attack. But the expected Confederate reinforcements never arrived; instead it was the Federals who rushed massive reinforcements to this dangerous break in their line.

The Southerners were soon driven off the hill and forced to withdraw back to Gettysburg, their bravery and sacrifices wasted.

This is a modern view of East Cemetery Hill, looking west from Stevens Knoll. The Evergreen Gatehouse can been seen at the top of the hill on the left. The Confederate battleline advanced from the town across that open field. First, they advanced in the direction of the camera, but then swung camera-left to face the Union infantry spread out along that road at the foot of the hill. Gettysburg lies just behind the treeline and was clearly visible at the time as the trees were much thinner back then. Note the undulations in the terrain. Fields are rarely as flat as they look on battlefield maps.

Photo 12A Gatehouse to Evergreen Cemetery
View looking SW. Photo taken by O'Sullivan, July 7th, 1863.

Photo 12B Gatehouse to Evergreen Cemetery
View looking SW. Photo taken by Brady & Co., around July 15th, 1863.

In 1854 the Gettysburg town-fathers selected a scenic and peaceful hill on the southeast edge of their growing town as the location for a new cemetery - Evergreen Cemetery - and the hill became known as Cemetery Hill and the ridge behind it became Cemetery Ridge. The gatehouse was built in 1855.

First Photo. Even today, everyone with a camera snaps a photo of the entrance to Evergreen Cemetery, and that was true for all the photographers who reached the field shortly after the battle. The first shot shown here, taken by Gardner on July 7th, 1863 at around 11am (judging by the shadows), just hours after the last units Army of the Potomac pulled out of Gettysburg in its pursuit of Lee's army.

In the photo, you can see the recently vacated artillery positions in the foreground - called "lunettes" - used in this case by Lt. James Stewart's Battery B, 4th US Artillery. Many traces of the lunettes can still be seen today.

Parked on the Baltimore Pike is a buggy of local sightseers who flocked to the field shortly after the battle. The town and it surroundings must have been quite a sight that day.

Second Photo. Brady and his camera crew reached Gettysburg about a week after Gardner and soon found their way to the gatehouse. One of Brady's assistants stands outside the gate in this photograph. Inside the gate entrance you can just see a Union soldier - probably a militiaman - getting himself

Photo 12C Gatehouse to Evergreen Cemetery
View looking SW. Photo taken by Tyson Bros. August, 1863. Photo owned by Gettysburg National Park

in the photo while apparently guarding the Gatehouse against scavengers.

Evergreen Cemetery is a civilian cemetery, as distinguished from the miliary or National Cemetery, which today is directly to camera-right of the civilian cemetery, separated by a fence. The military cemetery was created months after the battle when thousands of Union dead were collected from their hastily dug graves all over the battlefield, and brought to their final burial locations in the National Cemetery,

During the battle, Evergreen Cemetery was packed with Union artillery, which played a key role in breaking the desperate Confederate attacks on the evening of July 2nd in front of this Gatehouse.

On July 3rd these same guns swung around to the southeast and spewed death on Lee's massive assault against Cemetery Ridge.

Third Photo. This photo, owned by Gettysburg National Park, was taken a month after the battle by the Tyson Brothers. The cemetery caretaker and family lived in this Gatehouse, and over the years one side of the structure has been widened to add more living space. But even with the addition, the Gatehouse today remains in a remarkable state of preservation and is owned by the Evergreen Cemetery Association.

The cupola or bowl on top of the gate is black today. But the photos clearly show that it was white in 1863.

Photo 12D & 12E   Scene of attack by the Louisiana Tigers
View looking NE. Photographer unknown. Photo taken July 1863.

These two photos together form a panorama of Gettysburg which looks perfectly bucolic with horses grazing in the fields. You'd never guess that just a week or two earlier a furious battle was fought here.

At the end of the first day's fighting on July 1st, 1863, the Confederates occupied Gettysburg, which is visible in the distance. The Federals controlled East Cemetery Hill, from which this photo was taken. On the afternoon of July 2nd, Lee ordered what amounted to a "wave attack," beginning far to the south at Little Round Top and culminating here at East Cemetery Hill and farther west at Culp's Hill.

The top of Cemetery Hill was packed with Federal cannon. And there was another 6-gun Union battery on Steven's Knoll, a few hundred yards off camera to the right. The camera is located at the bottom of the Cemetery Hill, directly on this side of that road, known then as Brickyard Lane, and low brick wall you see in the photo. Union infantry stretched out camera-right and left in a battle line on this side of the road, guarding the base of the hill. The 17th Connecticut held the section of the wall directly in front of the camera.

The Confederates didn't begin their attack here until dusk. As you can see in the photo, the terrain toward Gettysburg was almost completely bare of trees at the

time. Two Confederate brigades emerged from the cover of town and that treeline on the left, and advanced in this direction.

Brig. Gen. Harry Hays' Louisiana brigade - known as the Louisiana Tigers - advanced toward the camera. Hays' line extended from the German Reformed Church (center background), across the rolling fields to a point directly in front of the Culp Farm (extreme right in the right photo).

To Hays' left, Col. Issac E. Avery and his North Carolina brigade advanced eastward across open fields for a time, taking tremendous artillery fire, especially from Stephens Knoll; but then, like a swinging door, the North Carolinians swung the left side of their line so that they faced this hill. They then attacked across an open field called Culp's Meadow, on the right of these photos.

The Confederates, about 3,500 rifles strong, advanced through a murderous artillery barrage, and then into sheets of fire from the Union infantry. But they broke the Union line in several places and some Southerners managed to make it to the top of Cemetery Hill, right in the heart of the Union line, and even seize some guns in savage hand to hand fighting.

(A Union prisoner, watching the attack from one of the town's church towers, later said of the Confederate attack that "I could see hands, arms, and legs flying

amidst the dust and smoke... It reminded me much of a wagon load of pumpkins drawn up a hill, and the end gate opening out, and the pumpkins rolling and bounding down the hill. "

A soldier of the 8th Louisiana said that once they reached the Union line [at that stone wall in the photo], "behind which the Yankees were, and here we had a hand to hand fight, the Yankees on one side and we on the other side of the wall - knocked each other down with clubbed guns and bayonets."

It was now almost completely dark. The Confederates on the hill were supposed to be reinforced by yet another attack on the hill from the west, commanded by Maj. Gen. Robert Rodes. But Rodes' attack got off late and quickly fizzled. With no help coming, the exhausted Southerners on the hill were forced to withdraw - their heroic effort and sacrifice, all for nothing.

When colorizing this photo, I noticed those bare spots on the far right of the photo with the two soldiers. A closer inspection shows posts, probably fence posts, standing randomly around the field near those bare spots. I can't think of any reason of why fence posts would be planted in a haphazard manner in a field. Maybe there's another explanation, but there's at least a possibility that those bare spots are the graves of Confederates killed in the attack. If true, this would be the first known discovery of Confederate graves photographed at Gettysburg

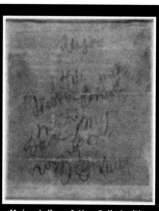

Major, tell my father I died with my face to the enemy.

I.E. Avery

Storming East Cemetery Hill on the left of the Louisiana Tigers was a North Carolina brigade commanded by Col. Isaac Avery. As Avery's men advanced across the open field of Culps Meadow under blistering cannon fire, Avery was struck in the neck. In the darkness and smoke his men didn't see him fall. As he bled out, he scrawled a note to his second in command:
"Major, tell my father I died with my face to the enemy.
I. E. Avery."

Col. Isaac E. Avery

Photo 12F   Union gun emplacements across Baltimore Pike from Cemetery Gatehouse
View looking NW down Baltimore Pike toward town. Photographer unknown. Photo taken July, 1863.

Here, the camera looks toward Gettysburg from the Evergreen Gatehouse, showing the interior of the artillery lunettes, constructed and occupied by Lt. James Stewart's Battery B., 4th US Artillery.

During the collapse of the Union line west of town on the first day, Stewart and his men held off the Confederate storm long enough to allow thousands of Union infantry to escape through the Oak Ridge railroad cut on the west side of town (Photos 2F and 3A). In the process Stewart lost two guns. He deployed the remaining four here, facing the town and guarding Baltimore Pike. You can see three of the gun positions in the photo; the fourth was on the opposite side of the Pike (left of the camera).

Also, note the stone wall on the horizon to the right. These were the lunettes Capt. Michael Wiedrick's Battery I, First New York Light Artillery. Wiedrick's position was temporarily penetrated by Louisiana troops of Harry Hays' brigade. The Confederates drove off Wiedrick's gunners in brutal hand-to-hand fighting. But soon Union infantry reinforcements arrived and eventually drove off the attackers in the darkness.

The sign in front of that big tent identifies it as an embalmer's operation. What looks like a strange little bearded man leaning against the fence post is actually a woman wearing the uniform of a vivandiere. Her name was "French Mary" Tepe and she was a member of the 114th Pennsylvania regiment. In the French Zouave tradition, vivandieres were females attached to regiments, providing the soldiers with various, generally legitimate, services, and tending the wounded.

In the earlier part of the war, both armies, but especially the Union army, were enamored with French Zouaves, which involved wearing gaudy, usually bright red and white, uniforms with baggy pants and turbans - all of which where totally impractical in the field.

"French Mary" Tape

Photo 12G View of Gettysburg from Cemetery Hill.
View looking NW. Photographers O'Sullivan and Gardner. Photo taken July 6 or 7, 1863.

This view of Gettysburg from Cemetery Hill, was taken by O'Sullivan on July 7, just four days after the battle.

This photo, taken just to the left of Photo 12F, captures Gettysburg as it recovers from the battle.

Here, the Baltimore Pike heads into town, though partially obstructed by a stone wall which, during the battle, had been extended across the road by Union soldiers as a defensive barrier against a possible enemy attack from the town. Just beyond that wall, parked along the opposite side of the road, is one of the two darkroom wagons used by Gardener's team in the field. Note the presence of the Wagon Hotel, situated near the bend in the road as it enters the southern extremity of town.

On the far side of Gettysburg looms the distant heights of Oak Ridge, and in the town itself the spires of the Francis Xavier Roman Catholic Church and the Adams County Courthouse (right) can be seen.

Those tents on the right belong to a northern militia unit that arrived in Gettysburg on July 6, the day before this photo was taken. With the departure of the last elements of the Army of the Potomac from Gettysburg before daylight on July 7th, the task of guarding the town and its recently established government facilities was assumed by these militiamen, who remained in Gettysburg for approximately a month.

Originals

12A

12B

12C

12D

12E

12F

12G

13 Cemetery Ridge

What Happened:

On July 1st, 1863, cavalry commander John Buford stalled the Confederate forces west of Gettysburg to buy time for the Union army to occupy the "good ground" south of Gettysburg. Well, Cemetery Ridge *was* that good ground.

Once the entire Union army deployed on Cemetery Ridge, its position was nearly impregnable. Unfortunately for the Confederacy, Lee convinced himself otherwise; he desperately wanted to take these heights, crush the Union army, and finish the war. Pure will power can sometimes achieve the impossible, but not in this case.

On the afternoon of July 3rd, after an hour-long Confederate artillery bombardment - the largest barrage ever seen on the American continent - 12,000 Confederate infantry stepped out of the treeline across the field on Seminary Ridge, bayonets gleaming and flags waving. On command, their lines swept forward like a machine, across the open fields under blistering Union cannon fire. As the shells, airbursts, and shrapnel screamed in and ripped gaps in their lines, the attackers simply closed ranks and kept coming. When they reached the fence at Emmitsburg Road, Union infantry opened fire.

On the northern side of the line where the road was still bordered by stout fences, many if not most Southerners took cover behind the fences as bullets whacked the rails like pelting rain. Only the bravest of the brave climbed the fences on both sides of the road and advanced up the hill toward Cemetery Ridge. But the bulk of the Confederate assault, led by General George Pickett's Virginians, struck at a location called the Bloody Angle, about 40 yards north of the Copse of Trees, the supposed original target of the attack.

One Confederate general, Brig. Gen. Lewis Armistead, leaped on the rock wall at the Angle, waved his sword and cried, "Give'em the cold steel, boys!" With that he leaped over the wall, followed by maybe 100 men. Armistead got about 10 feet inside the wall before he was cut down by three bullets, mortally wounded. All of those who followed him were killed or captured.

Within 15 minutes, perhaps 20, it was all over. The surviving Confederates sullenly retreated back across the field to Seminary Ridge, leaving half their number dead, wounded or captured on the field. When they reached Seminary Ridge, they surrounded Lee, mounted on his big gray, Traveler, begging for another chance to attack. But Lee would only say, "All my fault! All my fault!" And with that, the Battle of Gettysburg was essentially over, and the Confederacy doomed.

A modern panorama looking SW from Cemetery Ridge toward the Confederate position on Seminary Ridge. The Copse of Trees is on the far left. That lone tree in the center marks the Bloody Angle. Just to the right of that tree but in the middle distance is the Codori farm, and directly behind that, Emmitsburg Road. On July 3rd, 1863, the Confederate attack formation stretched almost the entire length of that treeline on Seminary Ridge.

Photo 13A   Cemetery Ridge and the Copse of Trees
View looking S toward the Round Tops. Photo taken by Tipton & Co., 1882.
Photo owned by William Frassantino.

This rather mundane photo has only one thing going for it - it's the earliest known photograph of the top of Cemetery Ridge and the "Copse of Trees," the probable aiming point of the final Confederate attack on the battle's third day. In what has to be one of the greatest blunders in photographic history, it wasn't until the 1880s, almost two decades after the battle, before any one bothered to photograph of Cemetery Ridge or the field of Pickett's Charge, the climactic battle of the Civil War. Why they neglected such an important spot is a puzzle; if for no other reason, the sweeping vista from the ridge should have attracted many a photographer's attention.

This 1882 photo was taken from a platform by William Tipton, and even then not because he considered the site particularly important, but because he had been commissioned to document the site for the construction of the Gettysburg cyclorama.

Photo 13B Looking at the Bloody Angle and Copse of Trees from Emmitsburg Road
View looking SE Photo taken by Tipton & Co., probably 1876-1877.

This is the earliest known view at close distance of the Bloody Angle on the left and the Copse of Trees on the right. Between them is the spot where Brig. Gen. Lewis Armistead of Pickett's Division called to his men to "Give them the cold steel," and leaped over that rock wall you see on the hill. Although he only get a few feet inside the wall before being cut down, his was the deepest penetration of the Union line that day, and so is known today as the High Water Mark of the Confederacy.

Even in 1877 the photographer, Tipton, didn't take this photo because of any particular interest in the Bloody Angle or the Copse of Trees. He included them almost by accident, because they happened to be there while he was photographing a series called "the ground occupied by the troops of Maj. Gen. Winfield Hancock during Longstreet's Charge."

The Copse of Trees was thought to be the unofficial aiming point of the final Confederate charge - the place where the attacking forces would converge. But the bulk of Confederate attack actually struck farther to the left, at the Angle, where two rock walls intersected.

Photo 13C On the field of Pickett's Charge
View looking S toward the Round Tops. Photo taken by Tipton & Co., probably 1876-1877.

As the title of this photo indicates, this was indeed the field over which Pickett's men charged Cemetery Ridge. The photo was taken about 13 years after the fact, but it's the first known photo of this field.

It was taken just before or after Photo 13B. Tipton simply swung his camera to the right.

The attacking Confederates advanced from camera-right to camera-left across the field on their way to Cemetery Ridge.

Photo 13D The Leister House - Meade's Headquarters
View looking N across Taneytown Road. Photo taken by Gardner, probably July 6th, 1863.

In 1863, in a two-room house that would probably fit into the closet of one of today's "MacMansion" houses, Lydia Leister was busy raising her six children - who ranged in age from 3 to 24 years old. She had purchased the nine acre farm just off Taneytown Road in 1861, two years after her husband's death, and supported her family working this tiny acreage, which included a small barn, orchard, and vegetable garden.

When the Union army arrived on July 1st, Mrs. Leister and her children were obliged, possibly ordered, to move into town with a relative. Gen. George Meade chose her house as his headquarters, as it was roughly in the center of his line and directly behind Cemetery Ridge (off camera to the left). After severe fighting on the first two days, it was at this house that Meade, who had only been in command of the army for a week, took a vote of his corps commanders, asking their opinions as to whether the army should stay and fight, or retreat. They elected to stay, with the expectation that Lee, having failed to crack either Union flank, would attack the Union center on Cemetery Ridge on the following day, which is exactly what he did.

The next day, shortly past noon, Meade and his staff were sprawled on the grass, having a pleasant lunch under the shade of Mrs. Leister's peach trees. One of the officers brought out a chair from the house to sit on, and the other officers teased him about putting on airs. Just around 1pm, the boom of a Rebel cannon at the Peach Orchard broke the silence. Then a pause. Then another cannon shot. Then all hell broke loose. Lee commenced his massive bombardment of Cemetery Ridge prior to the infantry assault.

Gradually, as the barrage continued, Confederate gunners began to overshoot the smoke-covered Cemetery Ridge, with the bulk of the shells landing behind the Ridge. That was fine for the Union infantry on the Ridge, but it was not fine for Meade, as he and his headquarters were in the bull's eye of the a rain of shells from over a hundred cannon. Meade and his staff hastily departed to another house on Taneytown Road, but for some reason Meade left one of his staff, Capt. William H. Paine, in charge of the building. The stalwart captain remained at his post throughout the tremendous cannonade, with many a shot plowing through the tiny house. Outside, 17 horses were killed. After the firing ceased, the captain was amazed to see several soldiers pop up from the cellar, where they had sensibly taken cover.

After the battle Mrs. Leister returned home, appalled to discover her yard littered with dead horses, her house riddled with artillery shells, her livestock gone, her crops and garden trampled, her fences destroyed, her food stores raided by hungry staff officers and headquarters guards, and her furniture dragged into the yard for use as writing desks.

Needless to say, she was not happy and she filed many a complaint over the years with the Federal government demanding compensation, but she never received any because most of the damage was caused by Rebel artillery, and the U.S. Government only compensated for damage done by the Union army.

She never got over the injustice of it, but the indomitable Mrs. Leister still managed to prosper. She purchased seven more acres of land in 1868, and added a large two-story addition onto the house in 1874.

In Photo 13D, taken three or four days after the battle, you can see some dead horses still lying in the middle of Taneytown Road, next to Mrs Leister's house.

In the photo 13E, taken four months later at the time of the National Cemetery dedication, the man standing on the porch, along with the two unknown children behind the blanket on the railing - presumably Mrs. Leister's - is Benjamin French, a passerby who just happened to be there when the photo was shot. He wrote that after the picture was taken he rode up Washington Street where in less than 10 minutes after he passed, a man and boy were unloading a shell when it exploded - the boy killed instantly and the man losing both arms and probably his eyes.

Back to Photo 13D for a moment, one interesting thing is that artillery of the time did not create shell holes. Mrs. Leister's yard looks almost unmarred. But those horses didn't die of old age.

Photo 13E   The Leister House - Meade's Headquarters
View looking NE. Photo by Gardner, Nov 20, 1863.

13A

Originals

13B

13C

13D

13E

14   The Cemeteries

Today there are two cemeteries on Cemetery Hill: one is the town cemetery, Evergreen Cemetery, which existed at the time of the battle, and right next to it is the Soldiers National Cemetery, dedicated four months after the battle.

Before departing Gettysburg three days after the battle, the Army of the Potomac only had time to hastily scape out some shallow trenches and cover the dead, many unidentified and their graves scattered all over the battlefield.

The various Northern states with dead on the field organized a movement to create a formal cemetery at Gettysburg and to reinter all the bodies there. The cemetery, which became a National Cemetery, was dedicated on November 19th, 1863 at a time when the reburials, and the war, were still very much in progress.

Almost as an afterthought Lincoln was invited to "say a few appropriate words." He arrived in Gettysburg by train the day before the dedication, and stayed that night at a house on the town square, the David Wills house, where he honed his speech - 278 words in ten sentences. The next day a procession with Lincoln and town notables in the lead, solemnly walked down Baltimore Street to the new cemetery. There, Lincoln would give his immortal Gettysburg Address.

Today, the bodies of just over 3,500 Union soldiers rest in the National Cemetery, over a third marked as *unknown*. With a few exceptions, Southern dead were never buried there. In the 1870s, the Southern states located and excavated about 3,200 bodies on the field, and reburied them throughout the South - with almost all of their graves marked *unknown*.

Over the years, the Park has opened "annexes" to the National Cemetery, where soldiers from more recent wars are buried.

Photo 14A   Dedication of National Cemetery as seen from Baltimore Pike
View looking SW from rear of Cemetery Gatehouse. Photo taken by P. S. Weaver, November 19th, 1863.

Here's a photo of the dedication of the Soldiers National Cemetery, taken from just inside Evergreen Cemetery, behind its famous gate, facing southwest.

At the time of the battle, Evergreen Cemetery had a sign announcing that any person caught discharging firearms on the ground would be prosecuted to the fullest extent of the law. This gave many Union soldiers a good laugh, and they mentioned it in letters home. That's probably the sign you see on the left of the photo.

The re-burial of the soldiers was far from complete at the time of this ceremony. In the photo you can see fresh graves in the right background. The grave appearing at the lower right probably contained the body of a Union soldier which would later be reinterred in his state's section in the cemetery. Samuel Weaver, the burial operations supervisor, didn't complete the reburial task until some five months later in March, 1864. In all, 3,512 Union bodies were transferred to their final resting place on Cemetery Hill, a third of them never identified. Weaver's company charged the government $1.59 per body.

Photo 14B   Dedication of National Cemetery
View looking NE toward the Cemetery Gatehouse. Photo taken by Gardner, November 19th, 1863.

This photo, taken from the opposite direction of Photo 14A, looks toward the back of the Cemetery Gatehouse. It's a shot of the crowd gathered to hear the cemetery dedication speeches, which included Lincoln's Gettysburg Address.

At the day of the dedication - November 19, 1863 - the guest of honor was Edward Everett, a famed orator; and he delivered a speech that ran a bladder-busting two hours - a customary length for formal speeches of the era.

Then Lincoln stood up, delivered his Gettysburg Address in two minutes and sat down again before any photographer could snap his picture.

Everett's voice was sweet and expertly modulated; Lincoln's was high to the point of shrillness, and his Kentucky twang offended many Easterners. But Lincoln had an instinctive feel for rhythmic delivery and meaningful inflections. His text was polished, and he was interrupted by applause five times. Contrary to popular myth, he didn't write the speech on the back of an envelope; it was written with great care back in Washington according to two witnesses, and he probably burnished it again and again on the train to Gettysburg, and in his room the night before.

If you visit the National Cemetery today, you'll see a massive Soldiers' Monument. But the speaker's platform - that rise in the photo - was not located where today's Monument sits. It was located about 40 yards east of the present monument, inside Evergreen Cemetery (the civilian cemetery) just behind a chain fence that separates the two cemeteries today.

Photo 14C Dedication of National Cemetery - looking toward speaker's stand
View looking SE. Photographer unknown. Photo taken November 19th, 1863.

In this photo of the National Cemetery's dedication, you see the large crowd gathered around the speaker's platform, visible in the rise to the distant left.

In the words of a witness: "Mr. Lincoln arose, walked to the edge of the platform, took out his glasses and put them on. He bowed to the assemblage in his homely manner and took out of his pocket a page of foolscap.

In front of him was a photographer with his camera, endeavoring to take a picture of the scene. We all supposed that Mr. Lincoln would make a rather long speech - a half hour at least. He took the singular sheet of foolscap, held it almost to his nose, and in a rather high tenor voice, without the least attempt for effect, delivered the most extraordinary address which belongs to the classics of literature. Mr. Lincoln finished before the photographer was ready. Very few heard what Mr. Lincoln said. The noticeable thing was the anxiety of all on the platform that the photographer should be able to get his picture. I remember we are all very much disappointed at his failure, and we were more interested in [the photographer's] adventure than in [Lincoln's] address."

The one photo taken of the event appears to be taken just as Lincoln sat down after giving his speech. Included here is a closeup of that photo, with Lincoln in the center.

Is there even one bodyguard there? Look how easy it would have been to assassinate him.

Peter and Elizabeth Thorn were born in Germany, but married in America. In 1855, Peter Thorn was appointed the first caretaker of Evergreen Cemetery. But in 1862, at the age of 35, he was mustered into military service as a corporal in Gettysburg's Company B, 138th Pennsylvania infantry. So for most of the next three years, Elizabeth Thorn assumed all the duties of the cemetery caretaker.

Six months pregnant at the time of the battle, she later described the flood of Union soldiers entering the peaceful Gettysburg township:

"On the morning of the first day of battle I was busy baking bread and was so occupied when the soldiers began to come up the Taneytown Road and through the cemetery. As fast as I could cut the hot bread they took it out of my hands and eat it. Every vessel I had in the house, all the tin cups and tumblers were out along the old pump inside the gate and the vessels were kept filled with water for the thirsty soldiers and were quickly emptied. They would take a drink and hurry off and this lasted until the pump broke."

Later: "While at the window I heard a soldier say that they ought to have a guide as they were killing their own troops because they did not know the country. Shortly afterwards a big man with straps on the shoulders came along and asked me whether there was a man who could point out the roads.

I told him my father was a German and he would not be understood and said I would go along and he replied there was too much danger for a woman. He insisted there must be a man somewheres to go along. I offered myself again. At last he said three times, if I was perfectly willing to go, I could. I thought there was as much danger inside as outside [the] house and so went along. He made me walk to the east or south-east of the horse to protect from any bullets. We walked through fields and came to where there were soldiers, who wanted to know what I was doing there. The officer said I was all right and the men gave me three cheers..."

Later in the day, after at least one shell had landed nearby outside and rocked the Gatehouse,

"I was in the basement when a man came in and asked whether I could make supper for General [Oliver O.] Howard. I told them I had no bread as I had given away all the bread baked that day to the soldiers, but could make some dough cakes and get them whatever was in the house. He laughed and said 'That was good enough for war times ...'

It was about sundown, and thinking Gen. Howard might come soon we got our supper and then let the supper table stand but they did not come until midnight and with Gen. Howard was Gens [Henry W.] Slocum and [Daniel E.] Sickles. ... When the three generals came

I was sort of taken back and said nothing while they eat..."

After eating, Slocum advised Elizabeth to stay in the Gatehouse that evening, but that he would send word if and when she needed to evacuate. He sent some soldiers to carry her family's possessions down to the basement as protection from possible shelling.

Early the next morning, July 2nd, a soldier appeared, informing Elizabeth that."This family is commanded by Gen. Howard to leave this house as quick as they can, to pick nothing up to take with them but their children." Elizabeth and her elderly father and mother stayed with some neighbors on Baltimore Pike. Later that night Elizabeth and her father returned to the Gatehouse to get some belongings, but were stopped. They were informed that there were wounded soldiers in the house and they should make no light as it might make the wounded soldiers restless. So Elizabeth went inside in the dark and came back with a shawl and a quilt. When she returned to the Gatehouse on July 7th: "Everything in the house was gone except three feather beds and a couple of pillows. The beds and a dozen pillows we had brought from the old country were not fit to use again. The legs of six soldiers had been amputated on the beds in our house and they [the beds] were ruined with blood and we had to make way with them." She found 16 soldiers and one colored man had been buried in her garden near the pump house.

She and her father dug 105 graves for soldiers over the next three weeks, for which they were never paid by the government, only her standard salary of $13 per month.

According to an interviewer, Elizabeth stated that "Whenever Gen. O. O. Howard returns to Gettysburg he never forgets the pleasure of a call upon Mr. and Mrs. Peter Thorn and recalls the midnight supper the lady gave him on the night of July 1, 1863."

Statue next to the Evergreen Cemetery Gate

14A

Originals

14B

14D

14C

Index

A

Adams County Alms House 35
Adams County Court House 25
Alabama; 4AL 44, 57; 15AL 45, 54; 44AL 58, 60, 61; 47AL 45, 54; 48AL 58, 60, 61
Anderson, Brig. Gen. George 40
Antietam 1
Archer, Brig. Gen. James 5
Arkansas; 3AR 40
Armistead, Brig. Gen. Lewis A. 97, 99
Armor, Robert D. 26
Army of the Potomac 1, 13, 18, 63, 103
Arnold, George 22
Avery, Col. I. E. 92

B

Baltimore Pike 31, 90, 94, 107
Baltimore Street 18, 23, 24, 30, 40, 103
Battlefield Hotel 30–38
Benning, Brig. Gen. Henry L. 40, 53, 54
Biesecker, J. 41
Bigelow, Capt. John 63, 64
Big Round Top 51, 54, 57, 58, 59
Blocher's Knoll 13
Bloody Angle, The 97–102
Boyer, Charles A. 21
Boyer's Grocery 21
Brady & Co. 8, 40, 41, 43, 84, 85, 86, 90
Brady, Matthew 1–2, 6, 8, 41, 43, 85, 90
Broadhead, Joseph 17
Brooke, Col. John R. 71, 74, 78, 79
Bucktail Brigade 5
Buford, Brig. Gen. John 3, 7, 14, 89, 97
Burns, John L. 14, 19–20, 35

C

Camp Letterman 16
Carlisle Street 22
Castle Monument 44
Cemetery Hill 3, 13, 26, 27, 30, 50, 89–96, 103
Cemetery Ridge 2, 9, 24, 39, 42, 43, 50, 54, 63, 66, 67, 69, 76, 83, 87, 89
Chamberlain, Col. Joshua L. 78
Chamberlin, Maj. Thomas 17
Chambersburg Pike 3, 6–7, 15
Chambersburg Street 19, 21, 22
Christ Lutheran Church 21, 22
Codori Farm 66
Colgrove, Col. Silas 87–88
Connecticut; 17CT 92
Copse of Trees, The 43, 97–102
Culp Farm 92
Culp, Henry 36
Culp's Hill 2, 36–38, 50, 83–88, 92
Culp's Meadow 92
Culp, Wesley 35–38
Culp, William 36
Custer, Brig. Gen. George A. 54

D

Delaware, 2nd 71–82
Devils Den 2, 40, 57, 58, 60
Dilger, Capt. Hubert 22
Dustman, C. Henry 14

E

Early, Maj. Gen. Jubal 17
East Cavalry Field 54
East Cemetery Hill 2, 8, 29–38, 89–96
East Middle Street 26
Emmitsburg Road 3, 13, 24, 32, 40, 63–70, 97–102
Essick, Rev. Abraham 27
Everett, Edward 104
Evergreen Cemetery 2, 32, 34, 43, 90, 91, 103–108
Ewell, Lt. Gen. Richard 9, 29

F

Fahnestock Brothers Store 23, 89
Farnsworth, Brig. Gen. Elon 54
Filby, Thaddeus 35
Forbes, Edwin 84
Frassantino, William 1, 6, 48, 53, 71, 74
French, Benjamin 101

G

Gardner, Alexander 1–2, 31, 48, 58, 59, 60, 61, 71, 76, 90, 100, 104
Gatehouse, The 90, 91, 103, 104, 107
Georgia; 2GA 54, 58, 61; 15GA 53; 17GA 49, 53; 51GA 71;

53GA 71
German Reformed Church 26, 92
Gettysburg Address, The 103, 104
Gettysburg College 9
Gibson, James 1, 44, 53
Granite Farm 54
Greene, Brig. Gen. George 83–88
Gutekunst, Frederick 2

H

Hagerstown Road 1
Hancock, Maj. Gen. Winfield 99
Hanover Road 36
Hardman, Pvt. Isa 15
Hays, Brig. Gen. Harry T. 92, 94
Herbst Woods 5, 8–12
Heth, Maj. Gen. Henry 3
Hewitt, Katherine May 51
Hill, Lt. Gen. A. P. 8, 9
Hood, Maj. Gen. John Bell 39, 44
Houck, John 40
Houcks Ridge 40–46, 47–56, 57, 58
Howard, Maj. Gen. Oliver O. 25, 29–38, 89, 107
Howell, Capt. Horatio S. 22
Humiston, Sgt. Amos 27

I

I Corps 9, 13, 31, 33
III Corps 39–46, 47, 50, 63–70
Indiana; 3IN Cavalry 15
; 27IN 87
Iron Brigade, The 5, 6, 18

J

Jackson, Lt. Gen. Thomas Stonewall 29
Jones, Brig. Gen. John 84

K

Kemper, Brig. Gen. James 66
Kershaw, Brig. Gen. Joseph B. 41, 79
Kilpatrick, Brig. Gen. Judson 54
Klingle Farm 66, 67
Knox, Thomas W. 86
Krauth, Dr. Charles P. 14
Kuhn, Mary 35

L

Lang, Col. David 67
Law, Brig. Gen. Evander 44, 54
Lee, Gen. Robert E. 3, 7, 10, 39, 54, 69, 71, 87, 90, 91, 97–102
Leister House 100, 101
Leister, Lydia 100, 101
Lincoln, Pres. Abraham 24, 32, 67, 103, 105
Little Round Top 2, 39–46, 47–56, 57, 58, 60, 61, 63, 83, 92
Longstreet, Lt. Gen. James 39, 40, 47, 69, 99
Louisiana Tigers 92
lum Run Valley 57
Lutheran Seminary 3, 6, 7, 13, 14, 15

M

Maine; 4ME 57, 58
; 20ME 44, 45, 78
Martinsburg, VA; 36
Massachusetts; 1MA 66; 2MA 87; 9MA Light Artillery 64;
13MA 21
McAllister, Mary 21
McClean Farm 13
McClellan, Georgia Anna Wade 34
McClellan House 34
McClellan, John Louis 35
McCurdy, Robert 22
McPherson, Edward 6
McPherson Farm 6, 17
McPherson Ridge 3, 6–7, 13
McPherson Ridge Railroad Cut 9
McPherson Woods 8–12
Meadee, Gen. 22
Meade, Gen. George 39, 47, 50, 63, 83, 89, 100
Michigan; 24MI 18, 23
Middle Street 26
Miller, Josephine 66
Mississippi; 21MS 63
Morrow, Col. Henry A. 23
Mudge, Lt. Col. Charles 87
Muhlenberg, Prof. Frederick 27
Mumper 24, 42, 66, 67, 69

N

National Cemetery 18, 24, 32, 48, 51, 103–108
National Museum of Health and Medicine 64
National Park Service 9
Negative Plate 2
Newman, Jesse D. 19
New York; 1NY Light Artillery 94; 4NY 61; 4NY Light Artillery 40, 47; 40NY 57, 58; 44NY 44; 60NY 84; 78NY 86; 97NY 15;

102NY 85
; 154NY 27
New York Herald 86

O

Oak Hill 3
Oak Ridge 3, 6–7, 9, 13–20, 94
Oak Ridge Railroad Cut 9
Ohio; 1OH Artillery 22
O'Sullivan, Timothy 1, 48, 49, 64, 65, 73, 75, 77, 78, 79, 90, 91
Oval Rock, The 74

P

Paine, Capt. William H. 100
Paine, Pvt. Lewis 67
Peach Orchard, The 2, 39, 40, 63–70, 76, 100
Pennsylvania; 21PA Cavalry 35; 28PA 36; 63PA 69; 83PA 44, 45
; 138PA 106; 143PA 6; 149PA 6; 150PA 5, 6, 8, 17
Pennsylvania College 23
Perrin, Col. Abner 8
Perry, Col. William 61
Pfiffer, Sgt. Samuel 8
Philadelphia 3
Pickett, Maj. Gen. George E. 66
Pickett's Charge 10, 98–102
Plum Run 41, 52, 54, 58, 60
Plum Run Creek 52
Plum Run Valley 40, 41, 47

R

Railroad Cut, The 6
Reed, Pvt. Charles 63
Reynolds, Maj. Gen. John F. 7, 14, 51, 89
Robertson, Brig. Gen. Jerome B. 41, 44, 53, 54, 57
Rock Creek 2
Rodes, Maj. Gen. Robert 93
Rogers, Peter 66
Rose Farm 71–82
Rose, John 71, 79
Rose Woods 40, 47, 75–82
Rupp, John 31
Russell, Judge Samuel R. 27

S

Schick Building 23
Schick, John L. 24
Seminary Ridge 3, 8–12, 13–20, 42, 75, 97–102
Semmes, Brig. Gen. Paul 41, 71–82
Shead, Louisa 15
Shead, Ms. Carrie 14, 15
Shead's School for Girls 14
Sherfy Farm 67, 69
Sickles, Maj. Gen. Dan 39, 47, 50, 63, 64, 69, 106
Skelly, Dan 14
Skelly, Jack 14, 35–38
Slaughter Pen 50, 51, 54, 57–62
Slentz, Mrs. Mary 17
Sletz, John T. 6
Slocum, Maj. Gen. Henry W. 83, 87, 106, 107
Slyder Farm 54–56
Slyder, John 54
Smith, Capt. James E. 40, 47, 61
Snow, Sgt. Archibald 22
Snyder, Catherine 31
Snyder, Philip 41
Soldiers Monument 104
South Carolina; 15SC 71
South Stratton Street 26
South Washington Street 33
Spangler, G. W. 24
Split Rock, The 71
Stearns, Austin C. 21
Steinwehr Avenue 31, 32
Stereoscopic Viewer 2
Steven's Knoll 92
Stewart, Lt. James 9, 90, 94
St. James Lutheran Church 27, 35
St. Joseph Central House 51
Stoever, Prof. Martin Luther 23
Stone, Col. Roy 5, 6
Stratton Street 27
Strong, Col. Vincent 44
Stuart, Maj. Gen. J. E. B. 3, 10
Swan, John 21
Swan's Grocery 21

T

Taneytown Road 22, 100, 106
Tate, Perry J. 14
Texas; 1TX 40, 49, 53; 4TX 44, 54, 57, 58, 61; 5TX 44, 54,

57

Thompson House 10
Thompson, Mary 10
Thorn, Peter 107
Tipton & Co. 98, 99
Tipton, William 98
Town Square 24–28
Traveler 97
Triangular Field, The 47, 49, 53
Trimble, Maj. Gen. Isaac R. 22
Trostle Farm 63, 64, 65
Trostle Lane 63
Tyson Bros. 2, 7, 14, 15, 16, 34
Tyson, C. J. 9, 21, 54

U

Union XI Corps 33
United States; 2US Sharpshooters 45; 4US Artillery 9; 4US
Light Artillery 90, 94
U.S. Sanitary Commission; 25

V

Valley of Death, The 40
Virginia; 2VA 36; 44VA 5; 55VA 5

W

Wade, Harry M. 35
Wade, James 35–38
Wade, Jennie 34–38
Wade, Mary Ann 35–38
Wagon Hotel 30–38
Walker, Brig. Gen. James 36
Ward, Brig. Gen. J. Hobart 40, 47
Warfield Ridge 39, 44, 75
Warren, Brig. Gen. Gouverneur 39–46
Washington Street 101
Waud, Alford R 60
Weaver Bros. 2, 22
Weaver, Peter S. 23, 50, 51, 103
Weaver, Samuel 103
Weikert, George W. 53
West Middle Street 23
Wheatfield Road 42, 43, 63, 69
Wheatfield, The 2, 39, 42, 57, 74, 83
Wheelock, Col. Charles 15
Wiedrick, Capt. Michael 94
Wilcox, Brig. Gen. Cadmus M. 67
Wills, David & Catherine 24
Wills House 18
Winchester, VA; 14, 36
Wisconsin; 7WI 6, 18
Wister, Col. Langhorne 17

X

XI Corps 13, 25, 27, 31
XII Corps 83–88, 87

Y

York Springs, PA; 27
York Street 27

Z

Zieglers Grove 43, 66

45922463R00069

Made in the USA
Middletown, DE
22 May 2019